A FalconGuide® to Saguaro National Park and the Santa Catalina Mountains

Help Us Keep This Guide Up to Date

Every effort has been made by the author and editors to make this guide as accurate and useful as possible. However, many things can change after a guide is published—trails are rerouted, regulations change, techniques evolve, facilities come under new management, etc.

We would love to hear from you concerning your experiences with this guide and how you feel it could be improved and kept up to date. While we may not be able to respond to all comments and suggestions, we'll take them to heart and we'll also make certain to share them with the author. Please send your comments and suggestions to the following address:

FalconGuides
Reader Response/Editorial Department
4501 Forbes Boulevard, Suite 200
Lanham, Maryland 20706

Or you may e-mail us at:

editorial@falcon.com

Thanks for your input, and happy trails!

*A*FALCON GUIDE®

Exploring Series

A FalconGuide® to Saguaro National Park and the Santa Catalina Mountains

A Guide to Exploring the Great Outdoors

Bruce Grubbs

FALCON GUIDE®

GUILFORD, CONNECTICUT
HELENA, MONTANA

A FALCON GUIDE®

All photos by Bruce Grubbs
Maps by Bruce Grubbs © Rowman & Littlefield.

ISSN 1555-4902
ISBN 978-0-7627-3419-1

Distributed by NATIONAL BOOK NETWORK

To my parents, who showed me the beauty of the outdoors.

Contents

Acknowledgments

I'd like to thank my editors at The Globe Pequot Press, Bill Schneider and Julie Marsh, for their patient work in making this a reality. Also thanks to Stephen Stringall, map coordinator at Globe Pequot, for helping me raise the maps to a higher standard. Thanks also to the personnel at Saguaro National Park and the Coronado National Forest who answered my questions. Finally, thanks to Duart Martin for her endless encouragement of this project.

Map Legend

Transportation

Interstate	(40)
US Highway	{26}
State or County	(23)
Forest Service Road	[089]
Interstate	≡≡≡
Highway	▬ ▬ ▬
Paved Road	▬▬▬
Gravel Road	═══
Unmaintained	= = = =
Featured Trail	▬ ▬ ▬
Trail	··········

Boundaries

Park/Forest Boundary	/////////

Hydrology

Dam	⌒
River/Creek	∿
Intermittant Stream	·-·-·
Spring	℘
Waterfall	∥

Physiography

Peak	▲
Valley	

Shaded Relief
used for overview maps

Arch/Cave	∧
Elevation Point	+
Pass/Saddle	)(

Symbols

Starting Point	🚶 START
Horse Trail	🐎
Parking/Trailhead	P
Picnic Area	⊞
Ranger Station	🏠
Restrooms	⊞
Visitor Center	？
Campground	⧊
Primitive Campsite	▲
Cabin	⌂
Point of Interest	■
Viewpoint	👁
Museum	🏛
City/Town	○
International Airport	✈

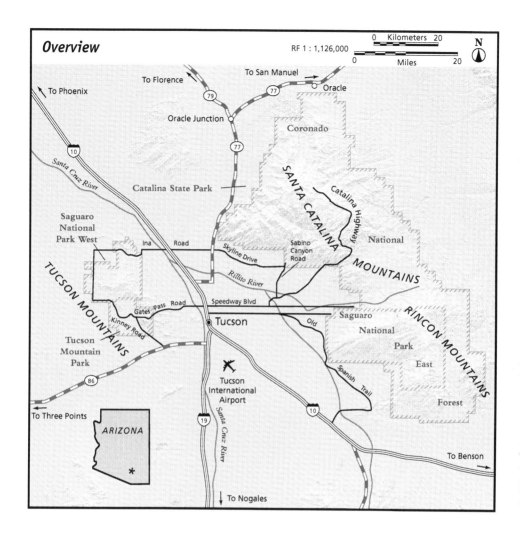

Overview

RF 1 : 1,126,000

Kilometers 0 — 20

Miles 0 — 20

N

To Phoenix

To Florence

To San Manuel

Oracle

79

77

Oracle Junction

Coronado

77

Santa Cruz River

10

Catalina State Park

SANTA CATALINA

Catalina Highway

National

Saguaro National Park West

Ina Road

Skyline Drive

Sabino Canyon Road

MOUNTAINS

TUCSON MOUNTAINS

Rillito River

RINCON MOUNTAINS

Gates Pass Road

Speedway Blvd

Kinney Road

Tucson

Old

Saguaro

National

Park

East

Tucson Mountain Park

86

Spanish Trail

Forest

To Three Points

Tucson International Airport

ARIZONA

19

Santa Cruz River

10

To Benson

To Nogales

Residents of Tucson are very lucky indeed. Not only is their desert city widely regarded as the cultural center of Arizona, Tucsonians who enjoy the outdoors are blessed with a national park literally at their doorstep. In addition to the east and west sections of Saguaro National Park, they can enjoy Tucson Mountain Park and the Santa Catalina Mountains, which are part of the Coronado National Forest, as well as the cultural features in and around Tucson.

Tucson occupies the valley of the Santa Cruz and Rillito Rivers, a broad desert basin between the Tucson, Santa Catalina, Rincon, and Santa Rita Mountains. This desert valley is also sometimes referred to as the Tucson Basin.

Saguaro National Park West, also known as the Tucson Mountain District, together with Tucson Mountain Park, encompasses a large portion of the Tucson Mountains, a predominately desert range that lies at the western edge of the city. Within the two parks are some of the finest examples of Sonoran Desert landscape in the Southwest, as well as large stands of giant saguaro cacti, the symbol of the Sonoran Desert.

Saguaro National Park East—also known as the Rincon Mountain District—includes most of the Rincon Mountains and is the larger of the two sections. The Rincon Mountains, which lie at the east edge of the city, rise more than 5,600 feet from their base to their summits. Because of this great elevation range, the Rincon Mountains feature four distinct life zones, ranging from desert scrub to fir-aspen forest. There are numerous isolated mountain ranges that reach similar elevations in southeastern Arizona, but the Rincon high country is one of the few that has no road access to the high country. The Rincons are the domain of the hiker, backpacker, and horseback rider.

At the north side of Tucson, the Santa Catalina Mountains rise even higher than the Rincon Mountains, and unlike the Rincons the Catalinas have a paved highway to the top of the mountain, giving easy access to campgrounds, trails, summer homes, rock-climbing crags, and even a ski area (the southernmost in the country). Luckily for the backcountry enthusiast, much of this complex range south and west of the Catalina Highway is included in the Pusch Ridge Wilderness, which is traversed by an extensive trail system.

In 2000 President Clinton designated Ironwood Forest, in the Sonoran Desert west of Tucson, as a national monument with the purpose of protecting ironwood trees and archaeological sites as well as a section of Sonoran Desert. Including the Silverbell, Waterman, and Sawtooth Mountains and portions of the intervening valleys, the monument encompasses 129,000 acres. There are no facilities, campgrounds, or trails, so the new monument is best suited for those willing to hike cross-country. Ironwood Forest National Monument is not covered in this book—for information, contact the monument at the address in appendix A.

Don't get the idea that Saguaro National Park and the surrounding area are just for the rugged backpacker and hiker. There are plenty of attractions for those who are more casual and don't consider themselves hikers. Tucson Mountain Park has an excellent, modern campground, popular with RVers, especially during the cooler half of the year. There are numerous commercial RV parks and campgrounds in and around Tucson. Tucson Mountain Park and both divisions of Saguaro National Park have scenic drives, and the national park has two visitor centers. The Coronado National Forest runs a visitor center at Sabino Canyon Recreation Area, and tram rides take visitors to scenic Bear and Sabino Canyons. The drive on the Catalina Highway from Tucson to Mount Lemmon is especially scenic. And the region has numerous cultural attractions such as the University of Arizona, the Arizona–Sonora Desert Museum, the Pima Air and Space Museum, the Tucson Botanical Gardens, and many others.

How to Use This Guide

This book is divided into four chapters, covering Saguaro National Park West and Tucson Mountain Park, Saguaro National Park East, the Santa Catalina Mountains, and finally, a chapter describing selected cultural attractions in and around Tucson. Each chapter except the Tucson chapter describes the park or forest unit in general terms, describes access to the park, transportation within it and how to find the trailheads, and includes a description of the visitor centers and other amenities, and campgrounds. The final portion of each chapter describes an introductory selection of hikes from very easy walks on nature trails to multiday backpack trips. The final chapter describes selected cultural resources in and around Tucson, organized alphabetically.

Mileages

Trail mileages are for the total distance of a hike. If the hike is out-and-back, that is, you return the same way you came, the total distance given includes the return hike. For one-way hikes, which require a car shuttle, the total distance assumes you will actually leave a shuttle vehicle at the end of the hike and do it one-way. Of course, if you do a one-way hike as an out-and-back, you'll walk twice as far as the total distance given. Loop-hike total distance is for the loop section that you hike one-way as well as any cherry-stem sections that are hiked out-and-back. Mileages were carefully measured with topographic mapping software. This was done for consistency, so that while the book's mileages may not always agree with official distances or trail signs, you can confidently compare hikes within the book with one another. In general mileages derived from mapping software tend to be slightly shorter than those measured on the ground.

Saguaro and ocotillo flowers. Usually, the saguaro blooms for only a single night.

Difficulty Ratings

All hikes are rated as easy, moderate, or difficult, a highly subjective rating that nevertheless should help you decide which hikes are for you. Generally, easy hikes are fairly short, can be done in an hour or two, and have little elevation change, so nearly anyone should be able to do these hikes. A few of these hikes are on smooth or paved trails that are wheelchair accessible; this fact is noted in the "Special Considerations" section of each hike. Moderate hikes are longer, take up to half a day or so, and often have significant elevation change, so you should be in reasonable shape for hiking, have good footwear, and have a pack to carry water and other essentials. Difficult hikes are long, taking most of a day or several days, and always have large elevation changes. Although none of the hikes in this book are cross-country, remember that trail conditions can change because of storms, wildfires, or just plain lack of use and maintenance. Check with Saguaro National Park or the Santa Catalina Ranger District of the Coronado National Forest for the latest information on trail conditions. For contact information, see appendix A at the back of this book.

Route Finding

Don't depend on trail signs for finding your way: Signs are often missing and sometimes inaccurate. While most of the trails described in this book were chosen because they are well used and easy to follow, there are many official trails shown on maps that are faint and receive little maintenance, as well as informal trails created by other hikers that may or may not know where they are going. Cairned routes, marked by piles of rock, should be followed with a healthy skepticism. Cairns are often constructed casually, with no thought to the overall route, and even by lost hikers!

Be responsible for your own route finding and don't leave it to others. Use a good map (see below) and keep track of your location as you go. You may even want to note your position and the time on the map occasionally. In any case, if you track your position faithfully, you'll never be puzzled when you reach a trail junction that has a confusing or missing sign. Tracking your location on a map can also help you judge your rate of progress, so you know when to turn back or when you'll arrive at a spring or planned campsite.

Also, decide on a baseline before venturing into the backcountry. A baseline is an unmistakable linear feature that forms a boundary along one side of your hiking area that you can hike to and be certain you won't miss. Roads are the best baselines, but you can also use large dry washes or even power lines. An example of a good baseline for hikes in the Tucson Mountains is Kinney Road, which runs along the west side of the mountains most of the length of the parks. A baseline is a last resort if you get completely lost and can't find the trail or retrace your steps. To hike to your baseline, all you have to do is hike in its general direction—in the case of the Tucson Mountains and Kinney Road, you would hike generally west. You can find the direction with the sun or stars, unless it is cloudy, but a compass is a much simpler method.

Always carry a high-quality compass—which is not the same as an expensive compass. Silva, Brunton, and others make basic, high-quality, liquid-filled compasses that cost very little. Although you won't often need your compass, when you do need it, you'll need it badly—in a heavy snowstorm, in dense forest, or on a desert flat in cloudy weather at night, for example.

Maps

The maps in this book that depict a detailed close-up of an area use elevation tints, called hypsometry, to portray relief. Each gray tone represents a range of equal elevation, as shown in the scale key on the map. These maps will give you a good idea of elevation gain and loss. The darker tones represent lower elevations and the lighter grays, higher elevations. The lighter the tone, the higher the elevation. Narrow bands of different gray tones spaced closely together indicate steep terrain, whereas wider bands indicate areas of more gradual slope.

Maps that show larger geographic areas use shaded, or shadow, relief. Shadow relief does not represent elevation: It demonstrates slope or relative steepness. This gives an almost 3-D perspective of the physiography of a region and will help you see where ranges and valleys are.

As mentioned earlier, all of the hikes in this book are on trails. The best map for Saguaro National Park is the National Geographic (formerly Trails Illustrated) topographic map *Saguaro National Park.* This excellent map accurately shows the trails, roads, and recreational facilities of both districts of the park as well as Tucson Mountain Park. It is available from Tucson outdoors shops, the park and forest visitor centers, and directly from National Geographic at www.nationalgeographic.com.

For trail hikes in the Santa Catalina Mountains, the best map is the *Pusch Ridge Wilderness* map, published by the USDA Forest Service and available from

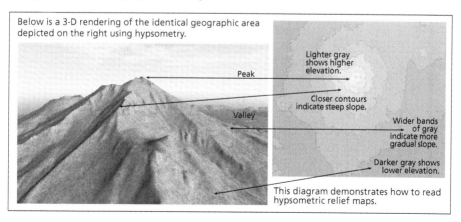

Below is a 3-D rendering of the identical geographic area depicted on the right using hypsometry.

Peak

Valley

Lighter gray shows higher elevation.

Closer contours indicate steep slope.

Wider bands of gray indicate more gradual slope.

Darker gray shows lower elevation.

This diagram demonstrates how to read hypsometric relief maps.

the visitor centers, outdoors shops, and directly from the Forest Service regional office at www.fs.fed.us/r3.

Those who wish to expand their exploration of Saguaro National Park and the Pusch Ridge Wilderness to the less-used trails and to cross-country travel and peak bagging will also need the 7.5-minute series of topographic maps published by the U.S. Geological Survey. These are derived from aerial photos and are extremely accurate when it comes to terrain and natural features, but because the topos, as they are also known, are not revised very often, trail, road, and other man-made features are usually out of date. Nevertheless, the 7.5-minute topo's fine depiction of topography is indispensable for the off-trail hiker, especially when used in conjunction with the two trail maps mentioned earlier.

Share the Trail

Most of the trails in this book are open to horseback riders as well as hikers, and some are open to mountain bikers as well. Horses always have the right of way over hikers and cyclists, both of whom should move off the trail downhill and remain still until the horses have passed. Talking quietly to the riders helps convince the horses that you are a person and not some weird monster with a hump on its back. Don't make sudden movements or noises.

Technically, hikers have the right of way over cyclists, but in practice it's more reasonable for hikers to step off the trail so as to avoid forcing the riders off-trail. On their part, cyclists should be courteous, always ride under control, and warn hikers of their approach.

Zero Impact

Being next to Arizona's second-largest city, Saguaro National Park and the Santa Catalina Mountains are heavily used. The backcountry can handle a lot more people if they work to minimize their impact. Most backcountry users probably don't intentionally abuse the land, thinking that cutting switchbacks on trails, dropping orange peels, building campfires, trying to burn their trash, picking flowers, and disturbing artifacts have no ill effects. But they do. Multiply each little impact by thousands of visitors, and soon the wild places look beaten down and hammered. Each visitor owes it to the thousands that will follow to have as close to zero impact as possible.

Three Falcon Principles of Zero Impact

- Leave with everything you brought in.
- Leave no sign of your visit.
- Leave the landscape as you found it.

Most of us know better than to litter—but how many people think of orange peels as litter? In the desert climate even organic litter such as orange and banana peels takes a long time to degrade. Tiny pieces of foil or paper from food wrappers may not seem like much, but they last for dozens of years and soon give the ground that littered, overused look. Likewise with cigarette butts. Consider picking up other people's litter on your way out. It adds little to your load and provides a great deal of self-satisfaction.

Stay on the trail. Cutting switchbacks actually costs more energy than it saves and leads to erosion and loss of vegetation. Most trail work is done by volunteers since land management agencies just don't have the budget these days to pay for trail maintenance. By cutting switchbacks you're just creating more work for a fellow hiker who's given up some of her hiking time to keep *your* trails in good shape.

Don't ever pick flowers or disturb artifacts, historical objects, or any natural features. Future visitors are entitled to appreciate these things, too. In the national park it's illegal to disturb or remove any natural feature, and in the national forest federal law protects both historic and prehistoric artifacts. Report any such disturbance to the nearest ranger station or visitor center.

Avoid making loud noises on the trail or at camp. You may be having a good time, but don't ruin other people's backcountry experience. If you have a dog with you, don't allow it to bark, especially in camp.

Remember that dogs are not allowed on trails in the national park. This rule protects wildlife from stress and harassment, as well as protecting your dog. In the national forest dogs are allowed on trails, except in certain areas that are closed to dogs to protect bighorn sheep or other wildlife. Dogs must be under control at all times. If your dog runs up to other people and doesn't respond to verbal commands, it is not under control and must be kept on a leash. Remember that every unpleasant dog-human encounter causes tighter restrictions on dogs.

When nature calls, use public restrooms at visitor centers, campgrounds, or trailheads whenever possible. If these facilities are present, it means that human use of the area is too great for natural disposal systems.

In the backcountry relieve yourself at least 200 feet from springs and creeks and away from dry drainages and washes. Even if surface water is not present, water is usually not far below the surface, and many dry streams flow for only part of the year. To take advantage of the natural, biological disposal system present in soil, find a site in organic rather than sandy soil if possible. Dig a cat hole about 6 to 8 inches deep, staying within the organic layer of the soil. Carefully cover the hole afterward. Some hikers carry a plastic trowel for this purpose. Pack out all used toilet paper and personal hygiene items in double plastic bags. *Never* burn toilet paper—numerous wildfires have been started this way.

Keep all camp waste, including toothpaste, dishwater, and soap, at least 200 feet from water. Never wash yourself or dishes in a spring or stream. Water is rare in this desert environment and all too easily contaminated. Rock tanks, also known as tinajas, are especially fragile and easy to contaminate. Remember that many other people will need the same water sources you use and that wildlife may also depend on them.

Camping in Saguaro National Park is allowed only at designated sites in the Rincon Mountains backcountry by permit only. There is a charge for permits, which are available at the Rincon Visitor Center or, well in advance, by mail. Camping is not allowed in the Tucson Mountain District of Saguaro National Park and all trails are day-use only. There are no vehicle campgrounds in the national park, but there is a vehicle campground in Tucson Mountain Park. Backcountry camping is allowed in the Santa Catalina Mountains and the Pusch Ridge Wilderness, and there are several public campgrounds along the Catalina Highway, at Catalina State Park, and elsewhere in the Santa Catalinas.

There is a fee for use of the Catalina Highway, which can be paid at the entrance station on the highway. Or, you can buy an annual pass to Saguaro National Park or the Santa Catalina Mountains. An annual National Park pass will get you into any national park or monument, while a Golden Eagle Pass is good for a year at all federal units—national parks and monuments, national forests, and other public federal lands. Annual passes cover entrance fees only, not campground or permit fees.

Strictly follow the pack-in/pack-out rule. Whether you're vehicle camping, day hiking, rock climbing, mountain biking, or backpacking: If you carried it in, you can and should carry it out.

Make It a Safe Trip

Although all three mountain ranges are located close to Tucson, you can be in isolated backcountry pretty quickly, especially in the Catalinas and Rincons. While this backcountry is as safe as any other, being prepared greatly increases your safety and that of your party.

Being prepared for a hike, rock climb, or bike ride is more than just filling your hydration bladder and blasting off. Give a little thought to what could happen. Changes in the weather, an injury such as a sprained ankle, losing the trail, or overestimating your party's abilities can turn an easy outing into a scary epic.

Know your limitations. Be realistic about your level of physical and mental fitness for a given backcountry trek. Allow plenty of time so you won't be stressed out trying to reach camp or a trailhead as the sun sinks to the horizon. Be willing to turn back if the outing is taking too long or a member of the group is having difficulty.

Mica Mountain from the Turkey Creek Trail, Rincon Mountains

Check the weather forecast. In these desert mountains an unusually hot spell can be as dangerous as an unexpected winter snowstorm. Late summer brings frequent thunderstorms with lightning, hail, and sudden heavy rain. Plan to be off high ridges and peaks by midday during thunderstorm weather, and never camp or leave a vehicle in a dry wash any time of year. Winter brings rainstorms to the desert foothills and snow to the high country, which can last for several days. Occasionally winter storms can be severe, with high winds and large amounts of snow.

Avoid traveling alone unless you are fit and experienced, and then always leave a detailed trip plan and your time of return with a reliable person who knows who to call if you are overdue. A trip plan is also a good idea with a group. Even if you're confident the group can handle an injury or problem, it's always comforting to know that help will come. I prefer leaving a copy of my map with the route and any planned campsites marked, as well as the location and description of my vehicle and license number.

Learn first aid and basic survival skills in advance.

Don't eat wild plants unless you know what you are doing.

Before you leave the trailhead, study the maps and learn as much as you can about the route. Plan your outing and know what time you have to turn back or be at the halfway point in order to return to the trailhead or reach a good campsite or spring before dark.

Keep track of your progress on your map, even if you're on an easy trail. That way you can never become lost. You also know whether you are making reasonable progress toward your goal.

Don't exhaust yourself or members of your party by traveling too fast. A group should move at the speed of its slowest member. Faster hikers can take advantage of the leisurely pace to look around or even explore side hikes. If anyone expresses reservations about the trail, route, ride, or climb, back off. And take plenty of rest breaks. Remember, you're out there to have fun, not to prove anything.

If you do get confused about your location, stop, sit down, have some water and munchies, and think about it. Chances are, all you'll have to do is backtrack a bit to find the trail. Note your present location, then scout back along the way you came, looking for the trail or trail markers. Leave someone at the point where you lost the trail as a reference point, and stay within sight or at least within earshot of that person. If you can't find the trail by backtracking, scout around your reference point in expanding circles. Have a look at your map and see if you can determine where the trail went. Never set off blindly cross-country without the trail, unless you are experienced and willing to commit to a cross-country hike. In the Catalinas and Rincons especially, you can quickly find yourself in extremely rough country, where progress may be slow or impossible. The old saw about following a stream downhill to civilization is problematic in this area because many canyons are blocked by impassable falls, especially at times of high runoff. In addition, the weather gets hotter and drier at lower elevations, especially during the summer.

In the rare case of getting completely lost or being stranded because of injury, storm, or nightfall, stay put, provide shelter for an injury victim and the rest of the party, and plan on sending two people for help as soon as it's safe to do so. Never leave an injured person alone, even in parties of two. Signal for help instead.

If you have a cell phone, try it, but don't count on it working. While you will probably get a signal on the high ridges above the city, deep in the canyons you won't. Be familiar with the traditional methods of signaling for help. Three of anything—three shouts, three blasts on a whistle, three columns of smoke or three fires, or three flashes of light—is the international distress signal. Mirror flashes are especially effective in sunny weather, when they can be seen 100 miles away. (During the Apache Wars, when the Indians cut the telegraph wires, the U.S. Army used mirror flashes and Morse code to communicate from mountaintop to mountaintop across the entire territory.) Practice with a signal mirror ahead of time, following the instructions that came with the mirror. The general technique is to focus through the sighting hole on your target, then move the mirror until there's a bright spot of sunlight on your target. This indicates that you're reflecting the sun directly at your target. Now, tap the mirror lightly to set up a flashing, twinkling appearance to the reflected sunlight so you'll catch the observer's eye. If the sun is low behind you, have someone stand in front of you with a second mirror and reflect the sun into your signal mirror. Signal mirrors are especially good for signaling aircraft.

Carry a basic first-aid, repair, and survival kit, containing at least the following: adhesive bandages, medical tape, gauze pads, a role of gauze, antiseptic ointment, moleskin, snakebite kit, sewing needle and thread, compass, whistle, signal mirror, flashlight or headlamp, lighter or other fire starter, water-purification tablets, a space rescue blanket, and a small booklet of first-aid and survival instructions. You should be able to treat minor injuries such as cuts or scrapes and blisters and stabilize victims with more serious injuries, as well as repair common problems such as failed stitches, broken buckles or straps, tears in pack fabric, and missing parts such as clevis pins, with your gear.

Avoid all wild animals. If you want to see animals close up, I highly recommend the Arizona–Sonora Desert Museum (see the Tucson chapter). Feeding animals causes them to become dependent on human food and lose their natural fear of humans, which could lead to a dangerous future encounter and result in the destruction of the animal. Any mammal can carry rabies. See the "Animal Hazards" section for more information.

Weather

Although all three mountain ranges are desert ranges, the higher elevations of the Rincon and Santa Catalina Mountains can experience significant, accumulating snowfall from November through early April, and occasionally even in October and May. At the highest elevations snow is possible any month of the year. Weather can change rapidly, especially during the winter and the late-summer thunderstorm season. There have been several fatal accidents in southern Arizona mountains when hikers were caught unprepared by a sudden or early-season snowstorm. Sudden heavy rains caused by thunderstorms can drop the temperature from a balmy eighty degrees F to fifty or lower in a matter of minutes.

The Catalina and Rincon high country is usually snowpacked for several months each year. Cross-country and downhill skiers, as well as snowshoers, can play on Mount Lemmon, the summit of the Catalinas, for several months most winters. When planning a winter or early-spring trip, remember that snow melts from south- and west-facing slopes first, and those are the slopes of the Rincons and Catalinas you can see from Tucson. North slopes often have much more snow, so much that you can be following a dry trail across a southwest slope one moment, then round a ridge onto a north slope and find yourself postholing through thigh-deep snow the next. Postholing may be good for building character, but it doesn't make for a fun hike unless you have skis or snowshoes.

Even the lower elevations of the Tucson Mountains occasionally get snow, though it normally melts in a few hours. Winter at the lower elevations is quite pleasant, and winter storms rarely last more than a day or two and are usually followed by several days or even weeks of sunny, mild weather.

The weather becomes more stable by mid-April, and the main threat is windstorms. If the winter precipitation has not failed, there will be an abundance of water in the canyons from snowmelt. Normally dry washes and streams are often running, and seasonal springs have water, which is a delight for day hikers and makes backpacking the wilderness much easier.

By mid-April the lower, desert elevations are starting to heat up, though you can do plenty of enjoyable hiking, biking, and climbing during the cool early-morning hours. In June, the hottest month, temperatures reach 110 degrees F in the desert, and 100 degrees is common up to 5,000 feet or so. At the highest elevations in the Rincon and Santa Catalina Mountains, 8,000 to 9,000 feet, June temperatures sometimes touch 90 but are usually in the 70s and 80s. In the dry air, temperatures drop 5.5 degrees F for each thousand-foot gain in elevation. When Tucson is frying in 100-degree heat, you can expect the temperature to max out at around 77 degrees F up on Mount Lemmon. That's why

Canada del Oro in flood, Catalina State Park

generations of Tucson residents have looked to the Catalinas for an escape from the summer heat.

Because of the drying effect of the spring winds and the hot desert sun, water starts to disappear from the mountain canyons by June. As the seasonal creeks and springs dry up, the delightful pools, waterfalls, and cascades vanish and trip planning becomes more difficult for backpackers.

July brings the North American Monsoon, a seasonal invasion of moist, tropical air moving northwest from the Gulf of Mexico. The main effect of the monsoon is to raise humidities from the usual teens or single digits to 50 percent or more, and to trigger almost daily afternoon thunderstorms over the mountains. These thunderstorms lash the mountain peaks and ridges with lightning and often bring short, heavy rains. Plan your outings to be off high peaks and ridges by midday during the monsoon. The sudden runoff from these storms can cause flooding in dry washes and canyons miles from the storm itself, which is why you should never camp or park a vehicle in a dry wash. As the monsoon gradually intensifies through August, thunderstorms may move off the mountains and bring heavy rain and dust storms to Tucson and the desert valleys. Rarely, an unusual surge of tropical moisture brings general rain to the region, lasting for several days. More typically, the monsoon follows a surge-and-break pattern, where several days or a week of daily afternoon thunderstorms are followed by several days where few storms form. Even during wetter periods of the monsoon, mornings are usually clear, with the first puffy cumulus appearing by late morning. In the mountains thunderstorms usually wind down by dark, leaving the nights clear and cool.

The monsoon usually ends about mid-September, bringing a change to clear, dry, cool weather. Though the lower desert elevations can still get pretty warm, hitting the eighties or even nineties F, the shorter days cause the nights to be cool or even cold. In the mountains autumn is clearly at hand; the aspens, maples, and other deciduous trees are showing their glorious fall color, and the mornings have a nip of frost. Since the abrupt heavy rains of the monsoon don't usually do much to restore seasonal creeks and springs, backpackers have to plan carefully around rare water sources, but the perfect weather more than makes up for the lack of water, especially for day hikers and mountain bike riders.

Heat and Dehydration

Summer heat is a serious hazard in the desert elevations. During hot weather it is safer as well as more enjoyable to hike early in the day, or at higher elevations, to avoid the afternoon heat. Always take plenty of water, even when the weather isn't scorching hot. The dry desert air, where the humidity often drops below 10 percent, causes insensible moisture loss from your skin and can lead to dehydration. People active in the desert often need a gallon or more of water per day. Sports drinks that replace electrolytes are also useful. Protection both from the heat and the sun is important: A lightweight sun hat is an essential, as are good sunglasses that protect your eyes from damaging infrared and ultraviolet radiation.

Prolonged dehydration and exposure to heat can lead to heat exhaustion, in which the body's heat-regulating mechanism begins to break down. Symptoms include weakness, pale, clammy skin, profuse sweating, and possibly unconsciousness. Move the victim to as cool a place as possible, provide shade and electrolyte-replacement drinks, and help the body's cooling efforts by removing excess clothing and providing ventilation.

If untreated, heat exposure can result in sunstroke, a life-threatening medical emergency in which the body's heat-regulation system stops working entirely. Sunstroke comes on suddenly and is marked by hot, dry skin as opposed to the pale, clammy skin of heat exhaustion victims. Additional symptoms include a full, fast pulse, rapid breathing that later becomes shallow and faint, dilated pupils, early loss of consciousness, involuntary muscle twitching, convulsions, and a body temperature of 105 degrees F or higher. Treat the victim immediately by moving him or her to a cool location, removing as much clothing as possible, making certain the airway for breathing is open, and using wet cloths or water to reduce body temperature. If cold packs are available, they should be placed around the neck, under the arms, and at the ankles, where blood vessels lie close to the skin. Transport the victim to a medical facility as soon as possible.

Hypothermia

Even in the summer, desert nights are cool, and in the mountains at higher elevations, nights can be downright cold. Temperature drops of fifty degrees F are possible during afternoon thundershowers. Winter storms can bring windy, rainy weather to the desert and blizzards to the mountains. Continuous exposure to chilling weather, during which your body is steadily losing more heat than it produces, can slowly lower your body temperature, resulting in hypothermia. Cool winds, especially with rain, are the most dangerous because the heat loss is insidious.

Hypothermia is a life-threatening condition. Its initial symptoms are subtle and can easily be missed by the inexperienced, but that is the stage where field treatment is the most effective. Episodes of shivering are the first sign that the body is losing heat—the shivering mechanism increases production of heat by muscle action. Although breathing and pulse usually remain normal during this stage, grogginess and muddled thinking are often present, which makes it difficult to recognize hypothermia in yourself. If a member of the party seems confused about where they are or the goal for the outing, be on the alert.

As hypothermia becomes worse, shivering becomes violent. This is the first sign that the body is losing control of its heat-producing mechanism. A marked inability to think and a short attention span along with slow, shallow breathing and a slow, weak pulse are serious warning signs. At this stage you have a medical emergency and the victim must be rewarmed with external heat, as his body is no longer capable of producing enough heat to warm itself. The best source of heat is other people. Ideally, someone should share a sleeping bag with the victim. Hot water bottles wrapped in clothing can be used, but care must be taken not to burn the victim, who can't sense when objects against his skin are too hot. Hot drinks can help but only if the victim is fully conscious.

Severe hypothermia is present when shivering stops, followed by unconsciousness, little or no breathing, and a weak, irregular, or nonexistent pulse. The victim's only hope of survival is immediate transport to a medical facility.

Clearly, prevention is the best treatment for hypothermia. It can be completely prevented by wearing enough warm and protective clothing to avoid chilling and by eating and drinking regularly so that your body continues to produce heat. During the winter or in the high country, be prepared for weather changes by bringing several layers of clothing, including wicking underwear, synthetic pants and shirts, a pile or fleece jacket, and a wind- and waterproof outer shell layer. Synthetic fibers such as polyester don't absorb water when wet and retain most of their insulating ability. In wet weather avoid cotton, which absorbs water like a sponge and dries very slowly. Rescue teams in the Pacific Northwest have a saying: "Cotton kills."

Water Purification

On day outings you should carry all the water you'll need. Backpackers who have to use backcountry water sources such as springs, natural tanks, and streams should always purify or filter all water before use. Purifiers, which include halide chemicals, some filter-based devices, and ultraviolet-light units, remove viruses as well as bacteria and cysts. Most filters do not remove viruses, but virus-borne diseases are fortunately uncommon in this area. Filters improve the taste of the water but are slow, heavy, and bulky compared to chemical purifiers. Keep filters clean by replacing the filter element or cleaning it per the manufacturer's instructions. Murky desert water has a way of clogging filters quickly, so use a prefilter if one is available for your unit.

When using chemical purifying agents, follow the instructions carefully, especially in regard to the wait time for the chemical to complete its work. Never add flavored drink mixes to water until the wait time has lapsed because the ascorbic acid (vitamin C) used in many drink mixes neutralizes the purifying agent.

Bringing water to a boil purifies it at any altitude but uses a lot of fuel and leaves you with a hot, flat-tasting drink. Pouring boiled water back and forth between two pots cools it off and restores the dissolved air that makes water taste better.

Old Mines

Old mines and prospects are common in these mountains. While hazardous areas are supposed to be signed and fenced, in practice this doesn't always happen, and some people ignore the warnings and get hurt or killed every year. Vertical shafts are a serious hazard, especially in brushy areas. Use a flashlight when walking through brushy areas at night off-trail, even around camp. Never approach the edge of a pit or shaft—the edges are often unstable or undercut and there's no way to tell how deep they are. Stay out of horizontal shafts and mines in general. They are often unstable, there can be partially covered or hidden vertical shafts, and poisonous or radioactive gases may be present.

Not all old mine shafts are fenced and signed like this one.

Cacti and Other Plant Hazards

The Sonoran Desert has a great variety of cacti, from tiny pincushions to the giant saguaro. All of them have spines. The spines on large cacti such as saguaro and barrel cacti are easy to see and avoid, but some are more subtle. Pincushion cacti tend to blend in with clumps of grass on rock ledges—scramblers and rock climbers should therefore watch where they place their hands. Most species of cholla cactus propagate by means of joints, the outer segments of branches that easily break off and cling to animals or humans that brush against them. Cholla cactus spines are fine, sharp, and microscopically barbed. You'll need a comb or a pair of sticks to dislodge the joints. Deeply embedded cholla spines, caused by falling on a cactus, may need pliers for removal. Dogs are especially adept at getting cholla spines deeply embedded in their mouths, which may require a visit to the vet.

Cholla spines, razor sharp and invisibly barbed

Plenty of other desert plants have developed spines for defense. Some agaves and yuccas have stiff swordlike leaves with sharp points that can do serious damage to the desert explorer unlucky enough to fall on one. Shin daggers grow in clumps at shin height and are thick enough to make cross-country travel difficult in some areas. Catclaw is a low bush that often grows in thickets and is covered with curved spines that catch on clothing and skin. All these sharp bits of plant tend to end up on the ground, so check the ground carefully before you sit down or set up a tent. Users of air mattresses and self-inflating foam pads have to be especially careful. Some desert backpackers have given up on self-inflating pads and use closed-cell foam pads instead, which aren't as comfortable but do have the advantages of being lighter and immune to punctures.

Poison ivy can sometimes be found along canyon bottoms and moist drainages at intermediate elevations, where it's often associated with the more common wild grape. The organic acid in the sap causes a skin irritation in many people. Both poison ivy and wild grape are low-growing plants. If you see wild grape, be on the alert for poison ivy. Learn to recognize poison ivy's distinctive glossy leaves, which always grow in groups of three. If you suspect you've been exposed, wash the affected area with soap and water, or just plain water, as soon as possible. Remember that dogs and pant legs can carry the sap to human skin as well. Calamine lotion is best for relieving the itching. Serious cases may require medical attention.

Chainfruit cholla

Animal Hazards

Rattlesnakes are common at all elevations in Saguaro National Park and the Santa Catalina Mountains. Many newcomers to desert hiking are scared off by the thought of being attacked by a rattlesnake, but rattlesnakes are not aggressive. They usually sense your presence before you are aware of them, and move quietly out of the way. If an intruder does get too close, or the snake is surprised or cornered, it uses its rattle as a warning well before you come in range of its strike.

The rattling sound, which the snake creates by rapidly shaking the rattle on its tail, is an unmistakable sound but one that can be difficult to locate, especially in grass or brush. When you first hear it, stop and locate the snake visually before moving quietly around it. Snakes sometimes den up together, so watch for other snakes as you avoid the first one. Never handle or tease any snake. Most snakebite victims are snake collectors, people working around rock or wood piles, and people playing with pet snakes.

Since rattlesnakes can strike no farther than approximately half their body length, avoid placing your hands and feet in areas that you cannot see, and walk several feet away from rock overhangs and shady ledges. Bites usually occur on the feet or ankles, so ankle-high hiking boots and loose-fitting long pants will prevent most injuries. Snakes prefer surfaces at about eighty degrees F. This means they like the shade of bushes or rock overhangs in hot weather, and in cool weather they prefer open, sunny ground. Don't confuse commonly found but nonpoisonous bull snakes with rattlesnakes—bull snakes don't have rattles on their tails.

Although rattlesnake bites are not life threatening except in rare cases usually involving the very young or infirm, the venom can do serious damage to tissue. Since the snake's venom is designed to immobilize mice and other small mammals that are the rattlesnake's usual prey, rattlesnakes usually save their venom for hunting strikes. Warning bites often inject little or no venom. Actually, the main hazards from most accidental rattlesnake bites are panic on the part of the victim and infection caused by the deep puncture wounds. If someone does get bitten, keep the victim calm and transport him to a medical facility as soon as possible. If possible, identify the snake but not at the risk of further bites. Rattlesnake bites can be identified by the two puncture marks from the venom-injecting fangs, in addition to teeth marks. Nonvenomous snakes can certainly bite you but do not leave fang marks.

Southern Arizona is home to another venomous snake: the Sonoran coral snake. Unlike its larger cousin, which is found in the southeastern part of the country, the Sonoran coral snake is too small to bite anything but possibly a finger. It's rarely sighted, but if you do see one, you can distinguish it from similar nonpoisonous snakes by its red, yellow, and black bands that entirely circle the snake's body. On nonpoisonous snakes with similar colors, the bands do not encircle the body.

Arizona's Sonoran Desert is home to one poisonous lizard: the Gila monster. This yellow, orange, red, and black lizard is about a foot-and-a-half long and is unmistakable. Although they are rare and protected by state law, if you do see one, don't be fooled by its torpid appearance. If molested, Gila monsters can react suddenly. Their venom is similar to that of a rattlesnake, but they grind it into their victim with hollow molars rather than injecting it with fangs. A Gila monster can be very difficult to remove and can do a great deal of damage, though the bite is not normally life threatening.

Mountain lions (also known as pumas or cougars) roam the Rincons and Catalinas and are occasionally sighted. More often you'll just see their tracks. There have been a few lion attacks on mountain bikers and runners in California and Colorado, where the big cats have apparently reacted to fast-moving humans as prey. Lions attack deer, their normal prey, by ambush and will not attack if at a disadvantage or outnumbered. That means that groups are safer than solo hikers. It also means you should make yourself appear as large as possible if you encounter a lion, by standing up straight, spreading your jacket wide, etc. Experts advise that you avoid eye contact and move away slowly. If attacked, fight back with anything at hand. Many lion encounters involve roam-

Mountain lion on exhibit at the Arizona–Sonora Desert Museum

ing dogs, so keep your dog on a leash. Remember, dogs are allowed only on roads in the national park, not on the trails.

Although grizzly bears have long been extinct in Arizona, black bears still roam the Santa Catalina and Rincon Mountains. While most are shy of humans, they are curious and may seek an easy meal. To avoid problems with bears, never cook in your tent or around your sleeping bag. In the backcountry use a long piece of nylon cord and a rock to hang your food, trash, and all items with an odor, such as sunscreen, insect repellent, lotions, and toothpaste, from a tree limb too weak to support a bear, well above the ground and well away from the trunk. Another technique that's useful where there's no suitable tree is to make a cache of your food, trash, and other items about 100 feet from camp, and then balance a couple of cooking pots on top. A bear-proof Kevlar food sack or plastic canister greatly improves the odds of keeping bears out of your food. The idea is that a bear will make a racket attempting to get into your food, waking you and hopefully scaring itself away. In campgrounds, stash such items in bear-proof boxes, if provided, or in your vehicle. Remember that your main goal is to keep the bears from getting the idea that campers are a meal ticket, not to protect your food supply for yourself. The worst case scenario for you is that you'll have to abort your trip—the worst case scenario for a bear is that wildlife managers are left with no choice but to kill it if it becomes a persistent nuisance and injures or threatens to injure someone.

Ringtail cats, raccoons, skunks, and mice are nocturnal animals that often become camp robbers, especially at heavily used campsites. All of them are persistent and can easily ruin your night's sleep. A bear-proof campsite box or portable bear-proof plastic container solves the problem, and a Kevlar bear sack at least slows them down. Food left in a vehicle is not safe from mice, as I found out the hard way when mice chewed their way through the ventilation ducts in my car, which was parked at a trailhead for several days with a plastic bag of tasty nuts sitting on the center console. When backpacking, hang your food if possible, and leave all pack pockets open so rodents can explore the enticing residual smells without having to chew their way in.

Mosquitoes are occasionally around in small numbers after snowmelt at the higher elevations. Spring rains can sometimes bring out a few mosquitoes in the desert. Because mosquitoes can transmit West Nile virus, use repellent and sleep in a tent when they are present. DEET in various concentrations seems to be the most effective repellent.

Scorpions are common in the Sonoran Desert, and one small species, called *Centruroides sculpturatus*, is particularly dangerous. Usually found clinging upside down to bark or rocks, this scorpion can be avoided by always watching where you place your hands and feet. Kick rocks and logs before picking them up, keep clothing and bedding packed or in a tent or vehicle when not in use, and always shake out clothing and footwear before putting them on. A sting from this scorpion is a medical emergency and the victim should get professional care as soon as possible. *Centruroides* has caused many more fatalities in Arizona over the years than rattlesnake bites, despite the fact that it is found only in the Sonoran Desert, whereas rattlesnakes are found statewide. More widely distributed and larger scorpions that are commonly seen walking upright on the ground are scary looking, but their stings are no worse than a wasp sting.

Africanized bees, originally released in South America, have spread north and are now well established in the Arizona deserts. These bees look identical to the common European honeybee but are more aggressive. Since they interbreed freely, even domestic hives can be Africanized. Avoid all concentrations of bees, especially hives and swarms. If attacked, drop your pack and run. Protect your eyes and don't swat at the bees. The smell of crushed bees apparently incites Africanized bees to attack more aggressively. Africanized bees won't pursue their victims for more than a half mile, and in fact, most victims have been old, infirm, or otherwise unable to escape. If shelter such as a building or vehicle is available, use it. Otherwise, try to get into brush or dense foliage, which confuses the bees.

Black-widow spiders, identifiable by the red hourglass-shaped mark on the underside, have a neurotoxic venom and can inflict a dangerous bite. At first the bite is not especially painful, but symptoms, which can include difficulty breathing, develop rapidly and victims should get medical care immediately. There is no specific field treatment; young children should be transported to a hospital as soon as possible.

The brown recluse spider inflicts a bite that is slow to heal and sometimes causes extensive tissue damage at the site but is not generally life threatening. Both spiders are more common around man-made structures such as woodpiles than they are in the wild. They like dark, hidden areas, so be especially careful picking up downed wood or rocks.

The dangerous-looking centipede can inflict a painful bite and can also irritate skin with its sharp, clawed feet, but it is not life threatening.

Kissing bugs, also known as cone-nose bugs or assassin bugs, are obnoxious insects that live in rodent nests and feed on mammal blood at night. The bite is painless and the victim is often unaware of the bite for several days, until a large, itchy welt develops. Kissing-bug bites usually heal in a week or so. Kissing bugs are not a problem during the cooler months, but during the warmer half of the year, they give desert backpackers one more reason to sleep in a fully closed net tent.

Ticks occur rarely in the desert. If ticks are discovered, though, do a careful full-body search every day. It's important to remove embedded ticks before they have a chance to transmit disease, which takes a day or more. Some ticks carry Lyme disease, which can cause complications if not treated.

People who have a known allergic reaction to specific insect stings are at special risk. Since this reaction can develop rapidly and be life threatening, such people should check with their doctors to see if desensitization treatment is recommended. They should also carry insect sting kits prescribed by their doctors.

Wildfires

Much of Arizona's forested high country has been affected by wildfires. These fires have increased in intensity and coverage in recent years. The Rincon and Santa Catalina Mountains are no exceptions. Several large fires have occurred in the Rincons, and much of the Santa Catalinas have been burned in just two recent fires. While the effects of these fires are not all bad, you can expect to

Old burn, Rincon Mountains

see areas of burned forest in the high country, as well as deadfall and trail erosion that may slow your progress. Since funds for trail maintenance are scant, it takes time to repair and reopen damaged trails.

Fire conditions have been made worse by a prolonged drought in the Southwest, as well as management practices that have increased the density of trees and underbrush. Both the National Park Service and the USDA Forest Service recognize that fire is a natural part of the forest and brushland ecosystems and use prescribed fire as a management tool to help restore the forests to a more natural state. When conditions are right fires are started in selected areas and monitored to see that they achieve the desired results. Lightning-caused, natural fires are often allowed to burn, especially in wilderness areas.

During extreme fire danger, which occurs nearly every year during May and June, areas of the park and the national forest may have campfire and smoking restrictions. When these restrictions are in effect, campfires may be permitted only in developed campgrounds or not at all. Although rare, areas may be closed to public entry when the fire danger is exceptional. Always respect these closures—rangers are reluctant to close the public lands and only do so when potential wildfires burn with explosive force and an extreme rate of spread. During such periods it is dangerous to be in the forest.

Even when fire danger seems low and fires are permitted, make certain your campfire is out and the ashes are cool to the touch before leaving. And never leave any fire unattended, even for a short time. Camp stoves, if properly operated, pose little or no fire danger.

Human History

Natives

The first people in the Saguaro National Park area apparently descended from those who migrated from Siberia to Alaska across the Bering Sea on a land bridge exposed by the lower sea levels of the Ice Age. Driven by climate change and population pressures, these nomadic peoples worked their way south and east, eventually occupying the entire North American continent. By 9500 B.C. bands of hunters were roaming the desert grasslands of southern Arizona, hunting mammoths and bison, as well as gathering plants. These nomads left little trace of their presence, aside from stone tools and animal bones.

As the climate continued to grow warmer and drier after the last glacial period ended, mammoths, horses, and camels diminished in numbers and eventually disappeared. To adapt to these changes, the nomadic peoples increased their use of plants. In particular, they discovered the high nutrition and usefulness of seeds, which were ground into flour with stone tools. These grinding slabs, called metates, consist of a large, flat base rock and a grinding stone. As the grinding stone is moved across the base rock, an elongated depression is worn in the base. The base rock is sometimes a large separate piece and sometimes just a depression in a large, immovable slab. At any rate, the use of metates marks the beginning of the Desert Archaic period, at about 7000 B.C.

Still nomads, the Desert Archaic peoples probably built temporary shelters and certainly had hunting camps that they used regularly, but most of the time they appear to have lived in the open. During the summer they collected cactus fruit and mesquite beans from the foothills. In the fall the wanderers moved higher in the mountains, collecting pine nuts, acorns, and other foods from the coniferous forests. Winter found them back on the desert floor, depending more on hunting as plant foods became scarce. Toward the end of the Desert Archaic period, corn appears to have been introduced from Mexico, and crops were planted in favorable areas with creeks or rivers. Still hunter-gatherers, the Desert Archaic peoples moved on while the corn grew, returning only to harvest it.

Around 300 B.C. the Hohokam peoples began to move into southern Arizona from Mexico, settling around the Salt and Gila Rivers in the Phoenix area. These two rivers flowed most of the year and were ideal for the Hohokam farmers, who needed reliable water they could divert to their fields. The Salt River Valley became the center of the Hohokam culture. Gradually, Hohokam made their way into the Tucson area by A.D. 200 and appear to have influenced the Desert Archaic nomads, who adopted some of the Hohokam lifestyle, including farming.

People began to live in small villages and built ditches and canals to water the Hohokam crops of corn, squash, beans, and cotton. Still, a significant portion of their food came from hunting and gathering wild plants. By A.D. 1250 some of the Hohokam had started building adobe houses, and within a few years some had adopted Mogollon-style adobe apartment-style buildings, influenced by people living along the Mogollon Rim in northern Arizona.

By about 1350 the Hohokam population was decreasing. A prolonged drought in the Southwest during the mid-thirteenth century may have been a factor, as well as overhunting. Gradually, the Hohokam stopped building complex adobe town houses and resumed living in the earlier village style.

When the Spanish arrived in the Tucson area in the mid-1500s, they found the Pima Indians living in a simpler style than the Hohokam did at the peak of their occupation. It's not clear whether the Pima are descendants of the Hohokam.

The Spanish

The first Europeans to see the area now included in Saguaro National Park were Spanish conquistadors, who rode up from Mexico City in the 1540s in their search for the rumored Seven Cities of Gold. What they found was a Pima Indian village, named "Stjuk-shon," at the foot of Sentinel Peak (now commonly known as "A" Mountain), an eastern outlier of the Tucson Mountains. When the Spanish eventually founded the Presidio San Augustin del Tucson, they apparently derived the name "Tucson" from the Pima name. As Stjuk-shon means "foot of dark mountain," the modern name seems appropriate. Because of attacks by fierce Apache warriors, the new settlement was built as a walled fort, like so many other Southwestern settlements. The design of the presidio led to Tucson's nickname, still in use today: "Old Pueblo."

In 1821 Tucson became part of newly independent Mexico, but life carried on much as before. There were farming and mining activities, but the marauding Apache, who strongly resented the European invasion of their homeland, made extended settlement difficult.

Northern Arizona and New Mexico were ceded to the United States after the Mexican War of 1848, but southern Arizona remained part of Mexico until bought as part of the Gadsden Purchase in 1854. Even when Americans arrived, they adopted many native, Spanish, and Mexican practices, which resulted in the interesting and varied cultural mix evident in the Tucson area today. More and more American settlers arrived, but the fierce Apache still made homesteading dangerous. The U.S. Army was making progress in controlling the tribes until interrupted by the American Civil War, when most of the Union troops were withdrawn to the East.

Confederate troops captured Tucson in February 1862, but Union soldiers were sent from California to deal with the threat. Arizona's only Civil War battle took place near Picacho Peak, northwest of Tucson, and Arizona remained in Union hands for the rest of the war.

Tucson was a wild place in the 1860s. Not only were the Apaches a constant threat, but there was little law enforcement, and most men wore guns on the streets of the town. Gunfights were common. Despite the Wild West atmosphere, Tucson prospered and served as the capital of the territory of Arizona from 1867 to 1877. The arrival of the railroad in 1860 really put Tucson on the map. Still, Arizona Territory was a wild place to attempt to make a living until almost the end of the nineteenth century, when the last Apache band under the famous leader Geronimo was finally subdued in southeastern Arizona.

Ranchers and Settlers

Arizona in general was not considered a prime place to settle because of the long, hot summers, and the territory grew slowly in the first half of the twentieth century. Electric pumps and deep drilled wells made irrigation of the desert more practical, and farming became a major factor in the Arizona economy. Copper also became a mainstay Arizona product, and rich deposits were worked in the area around Tucson. Miners and prospectors pushed into the surrounding mountains, looking into every canyon and hidden recess in search of valuable minerals. Such prospectors, along with ranchers, were probably the first people to explore the mountains around Tucson in detail. Traces of this old mining activity are evident today, especially in the most active areas such as the Canada del Oro, along the west side of the Santa Catalina Mountains, where gold was mined from the stream gravel using placer methods; the northeast ridges of the Catalinas; and in the Tucson Mountains.

Arizona Territorial University, the predecessor of today's University of Arizona and the territory's first university, opened in 1891. Statehood finally came to slow-growing Arizona on Valentine's Day 1912, the last of the lower forty-eight states to achieve statehood. Although the hot summer climate kept people from wanting to settle in Tucson, the mild winters were attractive to people from all over the world, who started coming to the area as an escape from the harsh winters back home. Some visitors stayed all winter, and the guest-ranch industry got its start. Now, winter visitors are a major part of the Tucson economy.

Tucson was an active participant in the oncoming aviation age, and what is now Davis Monthan Air Force Base started out as a civilian field to serve the developing transcontinental airline system. The Army Air Corps took over Davis Monthan Field at the beginning of World War II, and this military airfield was to play a major role in the wartime growth of Tucson.

After Pearl Harbor the military looked to the Southwest, with its clear, dry weather, as a place to train the vast number of pilots needed in the war effort. The wartime defense industry followed the army to Tucson, and many of the servicemen who worked or trained in Tucson returned to live here after the war. Widespread use of air-conditioning made the desert city a more attractive place to live, and Tucson began to grow rapidly, a growth that continues today. The city still attracts winter visitors from the entire planet, as well as increasing numbers of retirees fleeing from cold parts of the country. Tucson is now a major aerospace and high-technology center with a major airport, Tucson International.

Tucson Mountain Park

Residents of Tucson soon recognized how lucky they were to have such a variety of wildlands nearby. Pima County established Tucson Mountain Park in 1929 in the desert mountains to the west of the city. Originally 60,000 acres, part of the park was removed after protests by local homesteaders. Another large section of Tucson Mountain Park was added to Saguaro National Monument when the new national monument was created. Since then, additions have been made, bringing the current park to about 20,000 acres in size, covering the southern portion of the Tucson Mountains. Tucson Mountain Park remains an

Spring flowers, Tucson Mountains

important backcountry resource in the Tucson Mountains, with miles of hiking trails and a large campground, adjoining Saguaro National Park to the south.

National Monument to National Park

By the 1920s, extractive activities such as mining were changing the character of the mountains around Tucson, and cattle grazing and woodcutting were threatening the very existence of the giant saguaro cactus. Young saguaro cacti cannot stand direct sunlight, and most successful saguaro seedlings become established in the shade of nurse trees such as paloverde, ironwood, and mesquite. Mesquite and ironwood in particular make excellent firewood, a scarce resource in the desert, and cutting of desert trees for wood nearly eliminated the essential nurse trees. Even today most of the saguaros in the two divisions of the park are either very old, dating from before the establishment of the park, or very young, having got their start after grazing and woodcutting were stopped.

Saguaro National Monument was established in 1933 to protect these magnificent stands of saguaro cactus found in the foothills of both the Tucson and Rincon Mountains on either side of Tucson, as well as the other plants and animals of the Sonoran Desert. In 1976 Congress created the Saguaro Wilderness as a unit of the National Wilderness Preservation System, and most of both districts of the national monument were added to the new wilderness area. In 1994 the monument was upgraded to national park status. Roads have been built to the top of many of southern Arizona's mountain ranges, but thanks to protection as a national park and wilderness, the high country of the Rincon Mountains, which reaches 8,666 feet at Mica Mountain, is still the domain of the hiker and backpacker.

National Forest Reserve to National Wilderness

The Santa Catalina Mountains, north and east of Tucson, are the highest of the three ranges surrounding Tucson. (A fourth range, the Santa Rita Mountains, forms the distant southern skyline of Tucson and at 9,453 feet is slightly higher than the Catalinas. The Santa Ritas are much farther from Tucson than the other three ranges and are not covered in this book. See appendix B for guidebooks that cover this area.)

Originally called "Santa Catarina" by the Jesuit missionary Father Kino, who visited the area in 1667, the main Spanish interest in the mountains was mining. American miners concentrated on Oracle Ridge and the northeast ridges, where most of present-day mining activity is centered. Mount Lemmon—at 9,167 feet, the high point of the range—was named for Sara Lemmon, a botanist who discovered many new species of plants during an 1881 scientific exploration of the summit. Miners and other explorers established trails throughout the range, and until 1918 trails were the only way to reach the high country. In that year a road was pushed to the summit up the northeast side of the mountain from Oracle. Although it was a long trip by trail or road to the cool summit forests, early Tucsonians used the mountaintop as an escape from the summer desert heat.

In 1902 a national movement to conserve the nation's forest resources resulted in the establishment of the Forest Reserves, which included the Santa Catalinas. A few years later Congress created the present national forest system from the reserves, and the Santa Catalinas became part of the Coronado National Forest, under a new land management agency, the USDA Forest Service.

After World War II, as Tucson grew rapidly, demand for recreational facilities also grew. A paved road from Tucson to the summit, the Catalina Highway, was finished in 1952. Built mostly with prison labor, the scenic, winding road was the catalyst for rapid development of the mountain. The Forest Service, which had taken over the trail system established by miners and settlers, also built a number of campgrounds along the highway. The appropriately named town of Summerhaven, located near Mount Lemmon, became a village of summer homes and a conveniently located escape from the summer heat. Even a ski area was built, Mount Lemmon Ski Valley, still the southernmost downhill ski area in the country.

Growing public and government awareness of the value of undeveloped lands for recreation, preservation, and scientific research, spearheaded by several conservation groups, led to the passage of the Wilderness Act in 1964. Recognizing official wilderness as a place where man was a temporary visitor and nature would be essentially undisturbed, the act created a National Wilderness Preservation System with a number of areas protected immediately. Other areas have been added since, including the Pusch Ridge Wilderness, which was designated in 1978. The Pusch Ridge Wilderness includes most of the Santa Catalinas west and south of the Catalina Highway. As with other units of the national wilderness system, development is prohibited in the wilderness, and all travel is by foot or horse.

Natural History

The Sonoran Desert, in which Saguaro National Park is located, is the lushest of the four North American deserts and certainly one of the lushest in the world. "Lush" is not a word that comes to mind when thinking about a desert, but despite the arid and hot climate of the Sonoran that certainly qualifies it as a desert, it does contain an astonishing variety of plants and animals. This is primarily due to the fact that the Sonoran Desert has two wet seasons: the winter, when gentle rains of a day or two duration fall from December through March, and the late summer, when violent afternoon thunderstorms pound the desert with heavy, brief rains, typically lasting from July through about mid-September.

Turkey Creek Trail, Rincon Mountains foothills

Named after northwestern Mexico's state of Sonora, more than half the Sonoran Desert is in northwestern Mexico, but a significant portion is in Arizona, covering the southwest third of the state. That puts Saguaro National Park in the northeastern portion of the Sonoran Desert, which is the wettest and most diverse portion of the desert. Overall, the Sonoran Desert ranges from sea level to about 4,000 feet and averages about 2,000 feet, just below the elevation of the desert valleys in the Tucson area.

Why a Desert?

Deserts form because of a combination of factors, the most important being unusual heat and low precipitation. The Sonoran Desert lies downwind of the coast ranges of California and Baja California. Moisture-laden winter storms must cross these mountains before reaching the Sonoran Desert. Mountains cause the air to rise as it flows over their summit ridges, which cools the air and decreases its ability to hold water vapor. The vapor condenses in the form of rain and snow clouds, and much of the moisture contained in the storms is wrung out over the mountains. As the now-dry air descends the lee side of the mountains, it warms at a faster rate than it cooled when it was wet, so the terrain to the lee not only receives dry air but also warmer air. This "rain shadow" effect is most pronounced in the immediate lee of the mountains, and in fact the portions of the Mojave and Sonoran Deserts closest to the lee of major ranges such as the Sierra Nevada are the driest and hottest of the North American deserts. Farther east some moisture manages to make an end run around the mountains from the south, so winter storms that reach the portion of the Sonoran Desert in Saguaro National Park are not as dry. Other factors that have helped to create the Sonoran Desert are the sheer distance from the Pacific Ocean and the presence of cold ocean currents along the west coast, which modify the storm track.

Since the Sonoran has another moisture source, the North American Monsoon, which picks up moisture during the late summer and brings it northwest into Sonora, New Mexico, and Arizona, it has the benefit of two wet seasons more or less equally separated by dry seasons, unlike the Mojave and Great Basin Deserts, which lie farther west and north. So, even though the Sonoran is certainly a desert based on its annual rainfall, and especially when compared to moist, green portions of the continent, the two wet seasons allow it to have more diversity in plant and animal species than many people expect.

Geology and Geography

Most of the Sonoran Desert lies within the vast Basin and Range Geologic Province, which is characterized by broad valleys and more or less parallel isolated mountain ranges. It covers portions of Arizona, California, Nevada, Utah, and Oregon. Faulting caused by the stretching of the region on a continental scale causes some blocks of the Earth's crust to sink to form valleys while others rise to form mountains. The Tucson Mountains, Rincon Mountains, and Santa Catalina Mountains are all examples of such fault-block mountains. In southeast Arizona many of the isolated ranges rise to more than 9,000 feet, which is as much as 7,000 feet above the desert valleys below.

Volcanic rocks of the late Cretaceous age make up much of the Tucson Mountains, although there are outcrops of granitic rocks of about the same age at the northwest end of the range.

Granitic rocks of early Tertiary to late Cretaceous age make up most of the Santa Catalina Mountains and Rincon Mountains. While both ranges are rugged, with plenty of crags and rocky summits, access to the cliffs is easier in the Catalinas because of the Catalina Highway, which makes the range a favorite with rock climbers.

Erosion in the Tucson, Santa Catalina, and Rincon Mountains takes place because of running water, most of it occurring during rare heavy storms and during snowmelt. Even the 9,000-foot Catalinas weren't high enough to form glaciers during the coldest of the ice ages, but some of the granite outcrops in the high country are reminiscent of glacial forms found in more-alpine ranges. Unlike the northern portions of the Basin and Range Province, where all the runoff from the mountains collects in closed basins and evaporates before reaching the sea, the Sonoran Desert portion of the Basin and Range Province drains into rivers that, at least before man's intervention, did reach the sea. The mountains around Tucson all drain into the Rillito and Santa Cruz Rivers, which drain into the Gila River, itself a major tributary of the Colorado River.

Water, which has great carrying power as it cascades down the steep slopes of the mountains during storms, carries large amounts of sand, gravel, and rocks down the canyons. As the floods slow after exiting the mouths of the canyons, the water drops its load in a debris fan. The fans from the mouths of adjacent canyons overlap, forming broad-sloping skirts at the feet of the mountains. These are known as bajadas and sometimes extend for miles from the foot of the steep mountain slopes.

Life Zones

Because climate changes rapidly with increasing elevation—the air grows cooler and the high terrain attracts more rain and snow than the lower elevations—the plant and animal communities also change rapidly as you ascend. First studied by C. Hart Merriam in the mountains of northern Arizona, his concept of "life zones" identifies six distinct communities of plants and animals, defined by the dominant plants, as you ascend from the lowest elevations of northern Arizona to the highest. While Merriam's life-zone concept has since been modified to fit different theories and places, the original concept is still useful in visualizing the changes in plants and animals as you ascend the mountains. Saguaro National Park and the nearby Santa Catalina Mountains have four of the six Merriam life zones, lacking only the two at the highest elevations. Since temperatures are lower and moisture greater on north-facing slopes, the elevations of the life zones vary somewhat depending on exposure. You can see this effect even in small canyons, where the south-facing slope may be covered with semidesert grassland while the north-facing slope is covered with pine-oak-chaparral woodland.

The life zones found in Saguaro National Park are, in order of increasing elevation, Lower Sonoran, Upper Sonoran, Transition, and Canadian. The following sections describe the dominant plants and animals that inhabit each life zone.

Lower Sonoran (2,000 to 4,000 feet)

This is the life zone most visitors to Saguaro National Park encounter, and because of this I'll describe it in the most detail of the four life zones. It is dominated by saguaro cacti and many smaller cacti such as teddy bear, chainfruit, and staghorn chollas, prickly pear, barrel, and pincushions. Creosote bushes and bur sage are the most common shrubs, and paloverde and mesquite the most common trees. This makes the Lower Sonoran sound like a garden, and it is—as much as a desert can be—but the plants are widely spaced, with plenty of bare soil between. The dry ground can only support so many plants, and some, like the creosote bush, actually secrete inhibitors from their roots preventing creosote bush seedlings from sprouting too close to the adult plant.

Hidden just below the surface of the seemingly barren soil are millions of seeds waiting patiently for just the right amount of winter moisture. If these conditions are met, the desert will burst forth with an incredible flower show. Each spring, even in dry years, there are always some flowers to be seen.

Common reptiles include the western diamondback rattlesnake, the Sonoran gopher snake, the Gila monster, and many other species of lizards. The western diamondback is the largest of rattlesnakes, sometimes reaching 7 feet in length. Gila monsters are venomous lizards that reach about 18 inches or more in length. Rarely seen and protected by state law, these slow-moving reptiles can react suddenly if molested.

As you hike you will almost certainly flush a covey of Gambel's quail. The birds stay still under cover of brush until you approach too closely, then suddenly all take wing at once, right next to you. The mourning dove's distinctive sad song practically defines the sound of the Sonoran Desert.

While the fierce spines of cactus plants keep most animals at arm's length, not so with the cactus wren, which actually builds its nest in the spiny embrace of a cactus for protection against snakes and other predators.

Mammals that favor the Lower Sonoran include mule deer, coyotes, javelina, bobcats, several species of ground squirrels, and striped skunks. Coyotes are the song dog of the desert, often howling in packs just after sunset or, more commonly, during morning

Coyote on exhibit at the Arizona–Sonora Desert Museum

twilight. Javelina, or peccary, are wild pigs that live in small herds. Bobcats are about twice the size of a housecat but are rarely seen. Striped skunks, on the other hand, are all too common, especially around popular campsites, where they can keep you up all night with their attempts to rob your food bags.

Snowfall is rare in the Lower Sonoran, where most precipitation consists of rain, even in the winter. Occasionally, a few inches of snow will blanket the saguaro cacti, but the first touch of sun as the storm clears causes it to vanish.

Upper Sonoran (4,000 to 5,000 feet)

Only hikers can visit this life zone within Saguaro National Park, but those who drive the Catalina Highway pass through the Upper Sonoran during the first few miles of the highway's climb up the lower mountain slopes. A little bit more moisture and somewhat cooler temperatures help grasses grow on the southern exposures in the Upper Sonoran life zone. Saguaros can't withstand prolonged freezing temperatures, so they're absent here. The most common cactus is the lowly prickly pear, which is tough enough to handle the higher Transition life zone as well.

On north-facing slopes chaparral—a mixture of red-barked manzanita, scrub oak, and mountain mahogany—tends to form dense brush, which wildlife loves but is difficult to hike through. In Saguaro National Park pinyon pines and juniper trees begin to mix in with the chaparral as elevations increase.

Various lizards favor the Upper Sonoran grasslands, along with the black-necked garter snake. In the chaparral the Arizona mountain king snake is at home, as well as the Arizona black rattlesnake and the black-tailed rattlesnake.

Common birds include the rock wren and the canyon wren, with its distinctive song consisting of a long descending melodious trill with a "peep-peep" at the end. An even more melodious bird is the western meadowlark, which sits on high points and sings away for hours. American robins are also common during the summer.

Mule deer are joined in the Upper Sonoran by white-tailed deer, which flash their white tails in alarm when disturbed. Black bears roam this low in the wilder areas, and desert bighorn sheep are found in the most remote and rugged canyons.

The Tucson Mountains top out in the Upper Sonoran grasslands, and the transition between the Lower and Upper Sonoran is plain to see in the hike to the top of Wasson Peak.

Snow falls in the Upper Sonoran at least several times each winter but melts off between storms, except during unusual cold spells. Like the Lower Sonoran, most precipitation is in the form of rain.

Desert grassland, Upper Sonoran life zone, Rincon Mountains

Transition (5,000 to 8,000 feet)

Tall, stately ponderosa pines mark the Transition zone. This life zone and the Canadian above it don't exist in the Tucson Mountains, but ambitious hikers in the Rincon Mountains in Saguaro National Park East can explore delightful ponderosa glades in the high country around Mica Mountain and on the north slopes of Rincon Peak. Much of the highest country of the Santa Catalina Mountains is in the Transition life zone, which is traversed by the upper portion of the Catalina Highway.

Ponderosas have long needles in groups of three, and wind blowing through the treetops makes a softer sound than is usually associated with conifers. In their natural state, ponderosa forests are open, with large spaces between the trees. Various grasses and shrubs grow beneath the pines in patches.

At these mountain elevations, Cooper's hawks are joined by the tiny pygmy nuthatch, which can be seen traveling in large flocks. Pygmy nuthatches land in the tops of the ponderosa pines and work their way down the trunks, clinging upside down and pecking away at insects. White-throated swifts fly at incredible speeds, like tiny aerobatic jets, next to the cliffs where they make their nests.

Abert's squirrels, also known as tassel-eared squirrels because of the long tufts of fur on their ears, are hard to miss. A fairly large squirrel with a bushy tail that's as long as its body, the Abert's squirrel lives on ponderosa pine seeds. They've been known to drop green pine cones on unwary hikers below.

Snowfall is common during the winter in the Transition zone but sometimes melts off between storms on south-facing and lower slopes. Higher, north-facing slopes may have a snowpack all winter.

Canadian (8,000 to 9,000 feet)

Douglas fir, classified as a false fir because its cones hang down instead of standing up like true firs, appears in the Canadian life zone, usually mixed in with true firs such as white fir. Quaking aspen also joins the mix, especially in areas that have been burned or disturbed. On the Rincons, only the highest north- and east-facing slopes are in the Canadian life zone, while the Mount Lemmon area at the top of the Santa Catalinas has a larger Canadian zone.

Steller's jays are common in the Canadian as they are in the lower Transition zone. The adult males are deep blue with a dark crest on their heads, and they're often heard warning of intruders with a deep, unmusical squawk.

Raccoons join black bears and Abert's squirrels in this life zone, the wettest and coolest of the southern Arizona life zones. Up here, snow may fall any time of year and is usually on the ground from December through early April.

Ponderosa-pine forest in the Transition life zone, Rincon Mountains

Pine, fir, and aspen forest of the Canadian life zone near Spud Rock Camp, Rincon Mountains

Desert Adaptations

Just how do plants and animals manage to survive in an environment with as little as 5 inches of rain per year and summer temperatures that often exceed 110 degrees F? The answer lies in a remarkable series of adaptations made by the processes of evolution. Although I am primarily discussing life in the plains and foothills of the Sonoran Desert, life in the high country of the Santa Catalina and Rincon Mountains also has to endure dry conditions by the standards of more northerly forests.

Plants

Plants of the Sonoran Desert have adopted a variety of different and sometimes surprising methods of surviving and even thriving in arid conditions. Water is indeed the stuff of life: Most plants consist of 80 to 90 percent water and depend on it for the chemical processes, such as photosynthesis, that create food and sustain life. Water also supports plant structure by maintaining the shape and strength of cells and allows cooling by evaporation from the leaves.

One group of desert plants cheats a bit by growing near sources of water, usually along canyon bottoms emerging from the mountains, as well as around springs. Although the streams rarely run year-round (there are only two permanent streams in the area, both in the Santa Catalina Mountains), water often lies close to the surface even during the summer when the surface flow has disappeared. Plants such as Fremont cottonwood, Arizona sycamore, ashes, and various willows, which require large amounts of groundwater, take advantage of the situation and grow in ribbons along the streambeds and in clumps around springs. These "riparian" life zones are a special case, somewhat exempt from the normal climatic factors that have created the Merriam life zones.

Another group of plants avoids meeting the desert head on by remaining in the ground as seeds until conditions are favorable. These plants, technically annuals but better termed ephemerals, can wait as seeds for years until enough moisture comes in the form of winter or summer rains. When the conditions are met, the plants quickly germinate and often appear within a few days. Because the extra moisture is short-lived, ephemerals typically complete their entire life cycle in just a few weeks. These plants produce the glorious flower shows that occur some years and carpet the desert with millions of flowers, delighting the astonished visitor.

All is not as simple as it seems, because extra moisture alone doesn't trigger the germination of the ephemerals. Not only does a minimum amount of moisture have to fall, it has to fall in the right way. Gentle, prolonged rains are much more likely to trigger germination than torrential downpours. Temperature is also important. Plants that germinate during the winter need cool days and nights, but plants that grow following the summer rains need warm days and nights. So the Sonoran Desert plains and foothills tend to produce flower shows during early spring, while the less numerous mountain flowers tend to appear in late summer—August or even September—when the North American Monsoon has gained enough intensity to cover significant areas with rain. Contrast this with the post-snowmelt flowering season of more northerly alpine ranges.

The plants that most people think of as desert plants are the perennials, which face the desert through an entire year of extremes and may have to endure successive drier-than-normal years. Although even desert plants have their limits, most have a remarkable ability to endure long droughts. The ongoing extreme drought in the Southwest has shown just how tough the desert plants are. So far they have not died off in massive numbers like the pinyon pines, juniper trees, and ponderosa pines have at higher elevations.

Plants adapt to year-round life in the desert by either being drought tolerators or drought avoiders. The drought avoiders manage to avoid drought stress by either adopting extreme measures to conserve water—the water savers—or by being more efficient at collecting water—the water spenders. The savers conserve water by various methods. Some limit transpiration of moisture through their leaves by only allowing it to take place for short periods each day or with a waxy coating that slows the loss of moisture. Others reduce the surface area that they expose to the drying air. Some plants move or curl their leaves to avoid exposure to the sun during the hottest time of day, while others drop their leaves entirely during dry periods. Some plants can even partially die, dropping entire branches to conserve life in the remaining portions of the plant.

Water savers typically have extensive root systems, much larger than you would expect from the size of the above-ground plant. Some plants, especially cacti, even grow

Shin dagger and barrel cactus

special rain roots within a few hours after rainfall, increasing the plant's ability to quickly take in moisture from the soil before it disappears.

Cacti are among the best examples of water savers, capable of storing large amounts of water within their interior pulpy flesh. Saguaro and barrel cacti are prime examples. While the interiors of these plants are filled with soft pulp, their support comes from woody ribs that circle the plant below the skin. As the pulp absorbs water and expands, the ribs move farther apart. You can clearly see this effect from the outside. Saguaros in dry conditions have accordion pleats that are very close together, while plants that have received a moisture bonanza have pleats that are much farther apart, almost giving the plant a bloated appearance.

Cacti have other remarkable adaptations. Normally, green plants produce food by taking in carbon dioxide during the day and creating complex carbohydrates through photosynthesis with sunlight. But this means opening the plant's surface pores, which allows moisture to escape. Some cacti only open their pores during the night, when the humidity is higher and the temperatures are lower. They store the carbon dioxide as organic acids and then process it into carbohydrates during the day while the pores are closed.

Because water-saving plants expend water, and therefore energy, at a low rate, they are generally slow-growing, long-lived plants. A saguaro cactus may only grow a couple of inches during the first eight years of its life.

Water spenders take the opposite approach. These desert-adapted plants have the ability to extract more water from the soil than nondesert plants, so they can continue transpiration from their leaves even during the heat of the day. Like some of the water savers, many water spenders have large root systems. Some, like the paloverde and mesquite trees, reach far down to the water table. Another adaptation is the ability, even under dry conditions, to send new roots into moist areas. Even more remarkable is the fact that many water spenders can become water savers under prolonged drought, slowing down growth and waiting. Then, when wet weather finally does arrive, they grow at much faster rates than nondesert plants.

Drought-tolerating plants have the ability to survive far more moisture loss than comparable nondesert plants. Most shade plants start to wilt after only a 1 or 2 percent water loss, but drought-tolerant desert plants can withstand a 30 to 40 percent loss. Most of the adaptations that allow plants to endure drought are at the cell level.

The creosote bush, common in the Sonoran Desert and Saguaro National Park, is a fine example of a drought-tolerating plant. During extended dry periods the creosote bush sheds its mature leaves, as well as twigs and branches, but retains its small, young leaves. These leaves can lose 70 percent of their moisture and still be actively producing food for the plant. When moisture comes, the presence of the small leaves allows creosote bushes to take immediate advantage. Creosote bushes are so drought-tolerant that they grow in desert areas where it may not rain for a year or more and the summer high temperatures often exceed 120 degrees F.

Animals

Desert animals have a major advantage over plants: They can move to more favorable locations, whereas plants have to endure whatever conditions occur at the place where they took root. Animals can take advantage of microclimates—changes in temperature and moisture over distances of a few feet—to find more suitable habitat. The shady area under a bush may be dozens of degrees cooler than a patch of bare ground a few feet away. And the climate under a rock may be many times more humid than the top of that same rock.

Official desert air temperatures, measured at 5 feet above the ground, can vary from around 110 down to 60 degrees F during a summer day and night. At the surface, daytime temperatures can reach 155 degrees F, while at night, because the ground loses heat by radiation to the sky, temperatures can drop to 40 degrees F. Ground-dwelling animals such as snakes, insects, and rodents have to find some way to endure such extremes. The answer lies beneath the surface. Because of the insulating properties of desert soil, the temperature a couple of feet down only varies about 30 degrees F, and at about 4 feet there is no temperature change at all. By living at least part of the time in burrows, desert animals escape the temperature extremes and also have a more humid environment.

Some animals don't survive drought as individuals. Like ephemeral plants, they take advantage of wet periods to reproduce. For example, tadpole shrimp eggs can survive for years in the baked dry mud left after temporary rain pools evaporate. When the rain comes, the eggs hatch and the tadpole shrimp emerge to complete their life cycle before the pool dries up.

Many reptiles, such as snakes and lizards, are well adapted for desert life. Because they are cold-blooded, the body temperature of reptiles stays close to that of their environment. It's commonly believed that reptiles revel in the fierce desert heat, but in reality they would quickly die if left exposed to summer ground temperatures. Rattlesnakes, for example, function best at body temperatures around eighty-five degrees F, so they seek out places that are comfortable, such as shade on hot days and sunny rock slabs on cool ones. In extreme heat rattlesnakes retreat into burrows abandoned by other animals, where their low metabolic rates allow them to endure many days between meals. During prolonged cold temperatures, rattlesnakes and other reptiles become dormant, remaining in this state sometimes for months.

Although many desert reptiles will drink water when they have a chance, as a rule they get most or all of their water from their prey. In the case of rattlesnakes and other desert snakes, the mice and other small rodents that they eat provide most of their water. Desert tortoises, unlike most desert reptiles, are vegetarian, and they are capable of getting nearly all the water they need from grass and other low vegetation. Desert tortoises are active for about half the year, escaping the heat of midday in burrows that they dig. The winter half of the year is spent dormant in burrows.

The fringe-toed lizard has projecting scales on its hind feet that it uses to run across the areas of fine, windblown sand that it inhabits. This lizard often ends its run over the sand with a dive, burrowing rapidly into the cooler sand and continuing to swim under the surface for some distance. The fringe-toed lizard has overlapping eyelids and ear flaps to keep sand out, and special sand-trapping nasal passages allow it to breathe under the sand without getting sand in its lungs. The ability to swim under the sand not only keeps the lizard cool, it also hides it from predators.

The sidewinder rattlesnake has a unique method of moving on loose sand. As the name implies, this small rattlesnake (about 18 to 32 inches in length) moves forward by throwing its body sideways in a series of loops. It appears to be crawling sideways in a flowing curve. The tracks left are unmistakable: a series of parallel lines at an angle to the sidewinder's direction of travel. Not only is sidewinding an efficient method of movement in the sandy areas that sidewinders prefer, it also reduces the area of the snake's body in contact with the sand, helping to keep its temperature down.

Spadefoot toads carry dormancy to an extreme. Adult spadefoots spend most of the year dormant underground, waiting for the summer rains. Within an hour of the first heavy rain, the toads emerge into the temporary pools, calling to each other in loud bleats. After mating, the eggs are deposited in the temporary ponds, where they hatch in less than seventy-two hours. The hatchlings go through the larval stage in as little as ten days, and the adult spadefoot toads appear in time to burrow into the beds of the drying ponds. The name "spadefoot" comes from a sharp-edged projection on the rear of their hind legs, which they use to help dig backward into the mud as they bury themselves. If the summer rains fail, the spadefoot can survive another year.

Larger mammals and most birds can't use burrows to escape the heat. Birds, of course, have the advantage of wings. They can fly to cooler resting sites in trees or fly high above the ground where the air is cooler. One of the Sonoran Desert's enduring sights is that of the vulture or raven circling in updrafts thousands of feet above the ground, waiting patiently for some hapless rodent or reptile to lose its fight to survive. Flight also lets birds find springs or water holes at a distance, and some birds leave the desert entirely during the summer, migrating north to cooler climates.

Mourning doves, whose plaintive call is one of the Sonoran

Kit fox on exhibit at the Arizona–Sonora Desert Museum

Desert's distinctive sounds, live in the desert year-round. They can withstand an amazing 30 percent dehydration. They can also drink much saltier water than most birds.

Large mammals, though not as common as in wet regions, do survive and even thrive in the desert. Like birds, their mobility gives them an advantage over small mammals and reptiles in finding water. Desert bighorn sheep, which live in some of the most barren portions of the Sonoran Desert, are well adapted to desert life. Although the bighorns do need occasional access to open water, they do get a large amount of moisture from the vegetation they eat. Bighorn sheep prefer rocky mountainsides, where they congregate in small bands high above the canyon floors.

Jackrabbits have huge, heavily veined, thinly furred ears, which not only serve the usual rabbit purpose of listening intently for predators but also work as efficient radiators to help the animal lose body heat. Jackrabbits often come out in large numbers after sunset and can be seen jumping in front of cars on desert backroads, where they zigzag in confusion before dashing to safety in the roadside brush.

Kangaroo rats, which as the name implies get around by hopping on strong hind legs, can survive without any liquid water. Although many other desert animals can go long periods without a drink, most are dependent on water they extract from their prey or from succulent plants. The kangaroo rat actually metabolizes water from dry plant food and can survive completely without water.

The casual visitor to the desert looks at the stark, flat light of the hot midday sun and thinks that the desert is nearly lifeless. In reality, there is much going on beneath the surface, hidden from view. If the visitor spends some time in the desert, he or she soon learns that the desert seems to come alive at night, or after rains, or in cool spells, when desert life ventures forth.

Saguaro Cactus

Because the saguaro is a famous symbol of the North American desert and the primary reason for the establishment of Saguaro National Park, it deserves further explanation.

Saguaros are the largest cacti in the North American desert, growing as high as 50 feet. Their distinctive branched shape means "desert" to most people who see them, yet they only grow in one of the four American deserts, the Sonoran. Even within the Sonoran, the saguaros' range is limited to about half the Sonoran Desert, primarily in the Mexican state of Sonora and southwestern third of Arizona. Only a few saguaros grow in the California portion of the Sonoran Desert, and none is found in Baja California.

The saguaro cactus has a single main trunk, which is pleated like an accordion. The ridges of the pleats are covered with clusters of short, stiff spines,

Saguaro cactus "forest," Tucson Mountains

which effectively discourage most birds and animals from getting a meal. Vertical woody ribs underlie the ridges of the pleats and form the structural support for the plant, which can weigh seven tons or more. Of that weight, about 75 percent is water. Young saguaros have a single trunk, but when they reach about 15 to 25 feet in height and around fifty to seventy years of age, branches start to grow. The thick branches, structured exactly like the main trunk, grow horizontally for a foot or two, then grow upward. Sometimes many odd, close-spaced branches grow, forming a fanlike crest. Called "cristate" saguaros, there are only about twenty-five in Saguaro National Park. There is also one that can be seen on the nature trail behind the Sabino Canyon Visitor Center. No one knows why cristate saguaros form, but it may be caused by damage from a lightning strike or genetic mutation.

Saguaros start producing flowers at about thirty-five years of age. If winter rains have been plentiful and conditions are right, the saguaro flowers briefly in the late spring. Beautiful white flowers open at the tips of the branches and trunk and sometimes down the sides and are pollinated by insects, birds, and bats during the single night and day that they are open. The resulting fruits each contain thousands of tiny black seeds, which are an important food source for birds and other desert animals.

Even though a single saguaro produces many thousands of seeds, the plant will be lucky if a single seed survives to produce a new plant. Young saguaros require some protection in order to survive, so most successful plants get their start under a "nurse tree," a paloverde, ironwood, or mesquite tree that provides some shade, a cooler and slightly moister environment, and some protection from animals. Some research indicates that the saguaro may actually kill the nurse tree as it grows large and deprives the tree of water and nutrients.

One of the major reasons that Saguaro National Park was established was the rapid decline of new, young saguaros in the areas now protected by the park. Many years of woodcutting had removed many of the nurse trees, and the few unprotected saguaro seedlings that did manage to get a start were usually trampled by domestic cattle grazing in the desert. It became obvious that the magnificent stands of saguaros around Tucson were all older plants, and when they died the saguaro forests would be gone. Even today, many sections of the park have only very old or very young saguaros.

Without interference by man or unusually cold weather, saguaros can live to 150 to 200 years. They are defenseless against freezing and can't withstand prolonged temperatures below thirty-two degrees F. That limits the saguaros' growth on the mountainsides to about 4,000 feet, except on south-facing slopes where they may range a few hundred or a thousand feet higher.

Unlike some desert trees that have long tap roots that are able to reach deep groundwater, the saguaro has a large number of shallow roots that spread out

Saguaro cactus spines grow along the plant's vertical ridges.

radially from the base of the plant. During rain the shallow roots absorb water rapidly, and the plant stores this water bonanza against the inevitable long dry period. Since the moisture is stored in the pulpy interior, which expands as it absorbs more water, the diameter of the saguaro grows. The rib-and-pleat structure allows this expansion.

Many desert animals take advantage of the saguaro for food or a home. Gilded flickers and Gila woodpeckers both excavate nest cavities inside the saguaro, which doesn't permanently harm the plant. The saguaro heals the hole with a tough woody substance that often survives intact after the plant dies and the soft pulp decays. Known as saguaro "boots," these old nests can sometimes be found lying on the ground near the ribs of a long-dead saguaro.

Spring flowers in the Upper Sonoran life zone, Rincon Mountains

Elf owls, screech owls, purple martins, finches, and sparrows take advantage of abandoned saguaro nest cavities. Larger birds, such as red-tailed and Harris's hawks, build their nests of sticks among the arms of the older saguaros. Great horned owls and ravens may make use of abandoned nests.

The fruit of the saguaro provides nutritious food to animals and birds during the late spring. Under dry conditions, when easier and more succulent food plants are not available, jackrabbits, mule deer, pack rats, and bighorn sheep will sometimes eat the saguaro's pulp.

Saguaro National Park West

ying west of Tucson, Saguaro National Park West, together with Tucson Mountain Park, encompasses much of the Tucson Mountains. These desert mountains are the lowest of the three ranges covered in this book, culminating in 4,687-foot Wasson Peak. The foothills and south-facing slopes feature some of the best stands of saguaro cacti in the entire Sonoran Desert, while the higher ridges and peaks transition to desert grassland where smaller cactus are more common. The range runs generally north to south, but has several outlying portions. An extensive and popular network of trails covers much of the Tucson Mountains. Bouldering is popular among rock climbers, especially in the Gates Pass area.

Getting to the Park

Tucson is served by scheduled airline and bus service and is traversed by Interstate 10. Once in Tucson, you'll need a car to explore both national park districts and the Santa Catalina Mountains, since there is no public transportation to those areas. From I–10, which is east of the Tucson Mountains, there are three main access roads. The following directions take you to the Red Hills Visitor Center as a starting point for further exploration.

If coming from the north, exit I–10 at Avra Valley Road, turn right, and drive 5.1 miles west to Sandario Road. Turn left and drive 8.9 miles, and then

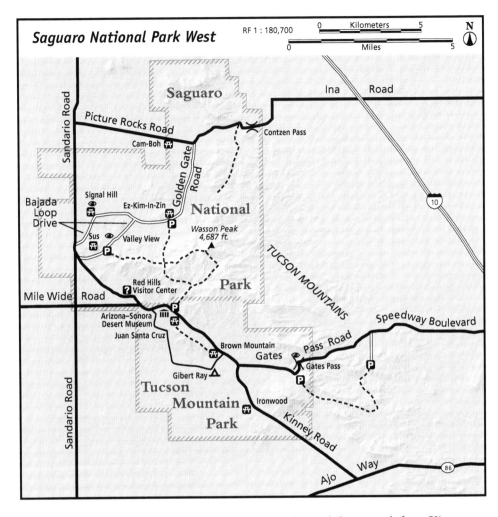

RF 1 : 180,700

Kilometers

Miles

N

Sandario Road

Picture Rocks Road

Saguaro

Ina   Road

Cam-Boh

Contzen Pass

Golden Gate Road

Signal Hill

Bajada
Loop
Drive

Ez-Kim-In-Zin

National

Wasson Peak
4,687 ft.

Sus   Valley View

TUCSON MOUNTAINS

Red Hills
Visitor Center

Park

Mile Wide Road

10

Arizona–Sonora
Desert Museum

Juan Santa Cruz

Speedway Boulevard

Pass Road

Brown Mountain

Gates

Gates Pass

Sandario Road

Gibert Ray

Tucson
Mountain
Park

Ironwood

Kinney Road

Ajo   Way

86

turn left on Mile Wide Road. Drive east 1.7 miles and then turn left on Kinney Road and drive 0.9 mile to the Red Hills Visitor Center.

From central Tucson, leave I–10 at the Speedway exit and drive 4.7 miles west on Speedway Boulevard, where it becomes Gates Pass Road. Stay on Gates Pass Road over Gates Pass (Tucson Mountain Park lies south of the road, and Saguaro National Park to the north) another 2.9 miles and then turn right on Kinney Road. Drive 4.7 miles northwest on Kinney Road to the Red Hills Visitor Center. Gates Pass Road is narrow and winding and not recommended for RVs and trailers.

From the south, exit Interstate 19 onto Ajo Way and head west 5.1 miles, where you'll turn right onto Kinney Road. Kinney Road passes through Tucson Mountain Park, then enters Saguaro National Park. After 10 miles you'll arrive at the Red Hills Visitor Center.

Getting around the Park

Kinney Road, running along and through the west side of Saguaro National Park West, is the main access route to the park.

The 6-mile Bajada Loop Drive can be reached by turning right on Kinney Road from the visitor center. This scenic loop on gravel roads traverses the desert foothills and also provides access to several trailheads and picnic areas.

South of the visitor center, Kinney Road provides access to more trailheads, as well as Tucson Mountain Park and its trailheads, picnic areas, scenic overlooks, and campground. Branching off Kinney Road in Tucson Mountain Park, Gates Pass Road winds over Gates Pass and passes several more trailheads and overlooks.

A few trailheads are accessible only by dirt road; these are described in the "Trails" section.

Finding the Trailheads

Because the Red Hills Visitor Center is centrally located and is an ideal place to start your exploration of Saguaro National Park West and Tucson Mountain Park, all trailhead directions start from there. Most trailheads are accessible from paved roads or graded dirt roads; a few are reachable only on rough roads.

Visitor Centers and Amenities

The Red Hills Visitor Center (520–773–5158; www.nps.gov/sagu) is the best place to become familiar with Saguaro National Park West. Exhibits, presentations, and guided walks explain the natural features of the park. A bookstore sells books and videos on the park and the deserts of the Southwest. You can also ask about weather and trail conditions.

The Arizona–Sonora Desert Museum (520–883–2702; www.desertmuseum .org), south on Kinney Road in Tucson Mountain Park, has an extensive exhibit of desert plants and animals and is well worth several hours or even a full day of exploration.

The International Wildlife Museum (520–617–1439; www.thewildlife museum.org) is on Gates Pass Road 5 miles west of I–10 and specializes in mammals, insects, and birds from all over the world.

Campgrounds

There are no vehicle campgrounds in Saguaro National Park West, but Gilbert Ray Campground is nearby in Tucson Mountain Park. The campground is open all year and has 149 sites, some with electric hookups. To reach it from the Red Hills Visitor Center, drive southeast 4.1 miles on Kinney Road and turn right at the sign.

Scenic Drives

HIGHLIGHTS: You'll pass through a fine saguaro forest and have access to picnic areas, a nature trail, and other short trails on this partially graded dirt but passable drive.

TYPE OF TRIP: Out-and-back.

DISTANCE: 9 miles.

This scenic drive starts at the Red Hills Visitor Center and winds through the foothills of the Tucson Mountains, passing though a fine saguaro forest. The drive is about 9 miles, including 3 miles of paved road and 6 miles of graded dirt road, portions of which are one-way. The dirt road is normally passable to all vehicles. There are two picnic areas, a nature trail, and several other short trails that are accessible from the scenic drive. In order to fully appreciate the Sonoran Desert, the drive is best done in the cooler weather of fall, winter, or early spring. If you do the drive in the summer, plan to do it early in the morning. Take a picnic and have a leisurely lunch at one of the picnic areas, and even if you're not a hiker, take a walk around the Desert Discovery Trail, do the very short walk to Signal Hill, or walk a few feet up one of the other trails. This is a general description of the scenic drive. For directions to specific trailheads, see the "Trails" section.

From the Red Hills Visitor Center, turn right on Kinney Road. The Desert Discovery Trail is on the left after 1.1 miles. Another 0.6 mile brings you to Hohokam Road. Turn right on this graded, two-way dirt road. You'll soon pass the turnoff to Sus Picnic Area on the left, and a little farther on, Hugh Norris Trailhead, on the right, where the road becomes one-way. After passing the Valley View Trailhead, the road continues to work its way up a valley through the desert foothills and then swings around the east side of Apache Peak, where it meets the Golden Gate Road. Turn left on Golden Gate Road, which is two-way, and follow it west around the north side of Apache Peak. After passing the turnoff to the Signal Hill Picnic Area and Trail, the road turns southwest and soon meets Sandario Road. Turn left on this paved road and continue south to Mile Wide Road. Turn left, drive to Kinney Road, turn left again, and continue to Red Hills Visitor Center.

Saguaro cactus "forest," Tucson Mountains

HIGHLIGHTS: On this drive you'll pass trailheads, picnic areas, the Arizona–Sonora Desert Museum, and scenic overlooks.

TYPE OF TRIP: One-way.

DISTANCE: 6.9 miles.

These roads provide the main access to Saguaro National Park West and Tucson Mountain Park, but they are also scenic drives in themselves. This drive takes you past several trailheads, picnic areas, a campground, the Arizona–Sonora Desert Museum, and numerous pull-outs and scenic overlooks, all on paved roads. Gates Pass Road is not suitable for trailers or motor homes—use the southern portion of Kinney Road instead. This is a general description of the scenic drive. For directions to specific trailheads, see the "Trails" section in this chapter.

Gates Pass, Tucson Mountain Park

From the Red Hills Visitor Center, turn left on Kinney Road. Just after Mile Wide Road comes in from the right, you'll pass McCain Loop Road, a scenic alternative to Kinney Road that loops around the west side of Brown Mountain. Continuing on Kinney Road, you'll pass the King Canyon Trailhead on the left, which marks the entrance to Tucson Mountain Park. The Arizona–Sonora Desert Museum is on the right, followed almost immediately by the Juan Santa Cruz Picnic Area. As you drive along the base of Brown Mountain, you'll pass several pull-outs and then the Brown Mountain Picnic Area at the southeast end of the mountain. Right after the picnic area, you'll pass the east end of the McCain Loop Road, which is also the access point to Gilbert Ray Campground. Stay on Kinney Road a short distance, and then turn left on Gates Pass Road. (Motor homes and other large vehicles should stay to the right here and follow Kinney Road south past Golden Gate Mountain.) Gates Pass Road heads east past several pull-outs, then passes David Yetman Trailhead (West), which is also a scenic viewpoint. A short section of very narrow, winding road leads to Gates Pass Overlook, one of the most scenic road-accessible places in the parks.

Trails

Picture Rocks Wash

HIGHLIGHTS: A hike through a beautiful saguaro cactus forest through Sonoran Desert hills, using the Ironwood Forest and Picture Rocks Wash Trails. These trails are in the northern portion of the Tucson Mountains, in Saguaro National Park West.

TYPE OF TRIP: Out-and-back.

DISTANCE: 5.4 miles.

DIFFICULTY: Easy.

PERMITTED USES: Hiking, horseback riding.

MAPS: Saguaro National Park National Geographic.

SPECIAL CONSIDERATIONS: During the hot summer months, plan to hike early in the day and carry plenty of water.

PARKING AND FACILITIES: The informal trailhead is a gravel parking lot on the north side of the road. There are no facilities.

FINDING THE TRAILHEAD: From the Red Hills Visitor Center, turn right on Kinney Road and drive 2.1 miles to Sandario Road. Turn right and continue 3.7 miles north and then turn right on Picture Rocks Road. Follow this road east 5.5 miles to the unsigned parking area on the left, just before the road goes over Contzen Pass.

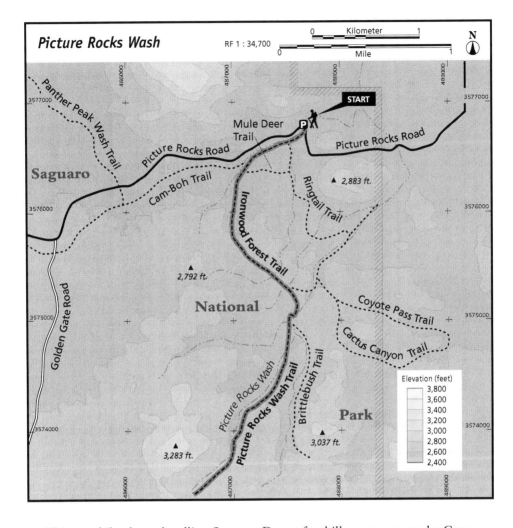

RF 1 : 34,700

Kilometer

0   1

0   1

Mile

N

Panther Peak Wash Trail

START

Mule Deer Trail

P

Picture Rocks Road

Picture Rocks Road

Saguaro

Cam-Boh Trail

Ringtail Trail

▲ 2,883 ft.

Ironwood Forest Trail

National

▲ 2,792 ft.

Golden Gate Road

Coyote Pass Trail

Cactus Canyon Trail

Picture Rocks Wash

Picture Rocks Wash Trail

Brittlebush Trail

Park

▲ 3,037 ft.

▲ 3,283 ft.

Elevation (feet)
3,800
3,600
3,400
3,200
3,000
2,800
2,600
2,400

This easy hike through rolling Sonoran Desert foothills starts out on the Cam-Boh Trail. Cross Picture Rocks Road and follow the trail down the wash. Almost immediately the Ringtail Trail forks left; stay right on the Cam-Boh Trail, which parallels nearby Picture Rocks Road. After 0.3 mile, turn left on the Ironwood Forest Trail, which heads south and climbs gradually through the low desert foothills. You are walking through the Lower Sonoran life zone, characterized by saguaro, cholla, and barrel cacti, green-barked paloverde trees, and creosote bushes. Watch for small saguaros nearly hidden in the shade of their nurse trees, usually paloverde. Paloverde trees have several adaptations to the hot, dry desert climate. Although the tree is seldom more than 10 feet high, its tap root can reach groundwater 100 feet or more below the surface. Paloverdes carry on photosynthesis in their green bark (*paloverde* is Spanish for

Desert wash in the Tucson Mountains

"green stick") most of the year. If the winter rains have been sufficient, paloverdes leaf out in the spring, taking advantage of the temporary moisture to put on a spurt of growth. As soon as the weather turns dry and hot, the tree drops its leaves, greatly reducing the amount of moisture lost via transpiration. After wet winters paloverdes are often covered with millions of tiny yellow or white flowers.

The Ironwood Forest Trail works its way into higher hills and finally climbs over a saddle and drops into Picture Rocks Wash, meeting the Picture Rocks Wash Trail. Turn right and continue past the Brittlebush Trail, staying in the wash on the Picture Rocks Trail to its end in the upper end of the wash.

Ironwood trees have, as the name implies, extremely hard wood. Popular with wood-carvers, the wood is also in much demand as an especially long-burning firewood, as well as for fence posts. In many portions of the Sonoran Desert, the ironwood has nearly disappeared. It is protected here in Saguaro National Park, as well as in the new Ironwood Forest National Monument.

There is a recurring myth that all deserts are shaped by wind. Although some are, the North American deserts, including the Sonoran, are shaped and eroded primarily by water. As faulting activity lifted the Tucson Mountains, running water tore them down. This process continues today. Most erosion takes place during infrequent heavy rains, which usually occur during the late-summer monsoon. Even though the ground is usually dry, it can't absorb heavy thunderstorm rains, which often fall at a rate of 2 inches per hour or more. The water runs off the bare ground between the widely spaced plants in sheets, carrying anything loose with it. Quickly the water gathers into small drainages, which in turn lead into larger drainages and eventually into washes such as Picture Rocks Wash. Flowing water's ability to carry silt, sand, pebbles, and boulders increases rapidly as the velocity of the flow increases, so major floods carry a load of sand and rock. These floods, sometimes more debris than water, act like giant rasps to wear down the beds of the washes and tear away the banks. Look closely at nearly any dry wash and you can see the signs of the last flood—undercut banks, debris piled in the trees and brush next to the wash, and dried potholes.

MILES AND DIRECTIONS

0.0 Start at the trailhead.

0.1 Stay right at the Ringtail Trail.

0.4 Turn left on Ironwood Forest Trail.

1.4 Turn right on Picture Rocks Wash Trail.

1.6 Continue past Brittlebush Trail, staying right on Picture Rocks Wash Trail.

2.7 The trail ends in upper Picture Rocks Wash.

5.4 Return to the trailhead.

Signal Hill Trail

HIGHLIGHTS: A short walk to a hill with a 360-degree view of the northern Tucson Mountains, as well as fine examples of ancient petroglyphs.

TYPE OF TRIP: Out-and-back.

DISTANCE: 0.4 mile.

DIFFICULTY: Easy.

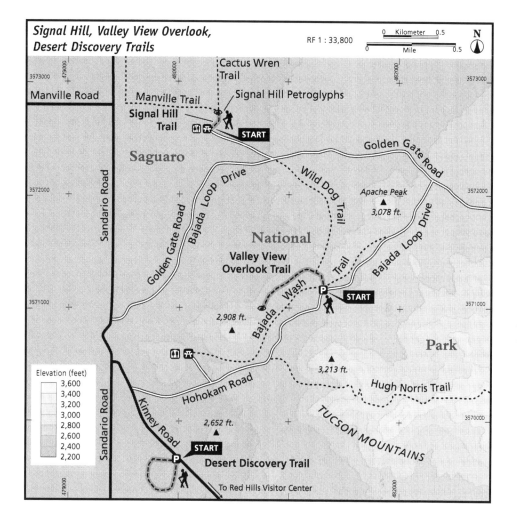

Signal Hill, Valley View Overlook, Desert Discovery Trails

RF 1 : 33,800

PERMITTED USES: Hiking.

MAPS: Saguaro National Park National Geographic.

SPECIAL CONSIDERATIONS: During the hot summer months, plan to hike early in the day and carry plenty of water.

PARKING AND FACILITIES: The trailhead is at the Signal Hill Picnic Area, which has restrooms.

FINDING THE TRAILHEAD: From the Red Hills Visitor Center, turn right on Kinney Road. After 2.1 miles turn right onto Sandario Road. In just 0.2 mile, turn right on Golden Gate Road and then drive 1.2 miles to the Signal Hill Road and turn left. Continue 0.4 mile to the Signal Hill Picnic Area and park.

Petroglyphs, Signal Hill Trail, Tucson Mountains

This very short trail leads to the top of a small hill with a fine collection of petroglyphs. There are two main types of rock art: pictographs, which are painted onto the rock, and petroglyphs similar to these, which are pecked or carved into the rock. Although some people have the impression that petroglyphs are casual doodling, stone is actually a difficult medium to work, somewhat harder than doodling on a pad of paper. The ancient artists had to pick the site carefully. They needed hard rocks with a solid coating of the dark desert varnish that forms after centuries of exposure to the relentless desert sun, and a location where the rocks would not be covered by floods or washed away. The care with which these people created their art is evident in its durability. How many modern artworks will last for centuries?

Looking around from Signal Hill, low though it is, your eye can rove over much of the Tucson Mountains. Apache Peak lies in the foreground to the east. To the southeast rises the long ridge that leads east to the highest portion of the range, culminating in 4,422-foot Amole Peak and 4,687-foot Wasson Peak. To the west lies the vast sweep of Avra Valley, much of it overlaid with farmland and houses. North of Signal Hill, virtually at your feet, lie several square miles of desert plain that is in its natural state, part of the Saguaro Wilderness and Saguaro National Park.

Valley View Overlook Trail

See map on page 61.

HIGHLIGHTS: A short walk to a ridge with a superb view of Avra Valley and Picacho Peak.

TYPE OF TRIP: Out-and-back.

DISTANCE: 1 mile.

DIFFICULTY: Easy.

PERMITTED USES: Hiking.

MAPS: Saguaro National Park National Geographic.

SPECIAL CONSIDERATIONS: During the hot summer months, plan to hike early in the day and carry plenty of water.

PARKING AND FACILITIES: None.

FINDING THE TRAILHEAD: From the Red Hills Visitor Center, turn right on Kinney Road. Drive 1.7 miles and then turn right on the Bajada Loop Drive. Continue 1.4 miles to the Valley View Overlook Trailhead, on the left. This section of the Bajada Loop is one-way; when you leave the trailhead, you'll have to turn left and finish the loop drive via Golden Gate Road to return to the Red Hills Visitor Center or to leave the park via Sandario Road.

From the trailhead, start on the Valley View Overlook Trail (the Bajada Wash Trail also starts from this trailhead), then walk 0.1 mile, passing the Wild Dog Trail. Stay left on the Valley View Overlook Trail and follow it another 0.4 mile to its end on a ridge overlooking the Avra Valley to the west and northwest.

This viewpoint is higher than Signal Hill and closer to Wasson Peak and the main mass of the Tucson Mountains. From such a vantage point, it is easy to see why the stands of saguaro cacti that stretch off in all directions are sometimes called a "cactus forest."

In the distant north, look for a sharp, isolated peak—it's Picacho Peak, site of Arizona's only Civil War battle. *Picacho* means "peak" in Spanish, so the Anglicized name is somewhat redundant.

Isolated desert mountains such as Picacho Peak and others that you can see from this viewpoint are the remains of desert ranges that are nearly eroded away. Early in their lives, fault-block mountains form a long, narrow, continuous range. As occasional heavy storms erode the mountains, debris is carried down the steep slopes to the foothills and then out into the desert valleys along washes. Gradually the mountains are worn down, and at the same time the valleys fill with this alluvial debris, burying the mountains in their own detritus and leaving isolated remnants of the mountains standing alone on the plains.

MILES AND DIRECTIONS

0.0 Begin at the Valley View Overlook Trailhead.

0.1 Pass Wild Dog Trail, staying left on Valley View Overlook Trail.

0.5 Arrive at the viewpoint.

1.0 Return to the Valley View Overlook Trailhead.

Desert Discovery Trail

See map on page 61.

HIGHLIGHTS: A wheelchair-accessible nature trail that loops through the desert south of Kinney Road.

TYPE OF TRIP: Loop.

DISTANCE: 0.4 mile.

DIFFICULTY: Easy.

PERMITTED USES: Hiking.

MAPS: Saguaro National Park National Geographic.

SPECIAL CONSIDERATIONS: None.

PARKING AND FACILITIES: Paved parking; trail is wheelchair accessible.

FINDING THE TRAILHEAD: From the Red Hills Visitor Center, turn right on Kinney Road and drive 1.1 miles to the Desert Discovery Trailhead, which is on the left.

This self-guided nature trail loops through a small section of desert plains and features small signs that inform you about the plants and animals of the Sonoran Desert. Look for several examples of dead and fallen saguaros, which reveal their inner structure. Unlike trees, saguaros are supported by a ring of woody, individual ribs just under the outer skin of the plant. The interior consists of a moist pulp, which is protected by the ribs. Unlike some desert plants, saguaros

Downed saguaro, Desert Discovery Trail, Tucson Mountains

do not use deep groundwater to survive dry periods. Instead, these huge cacti have a shallow root system that collects water rapidly after rains. The entire plant expands as it stores water and gradually contracts as internal moisture is used.

Because the shallow root system is incapable of supporting the plant, saguaros are literally balanced on their bases, which some people have found out the hard way after vandalizing a saguaro. In at least one highly publicized case, someone shot at a saguaro with a shotgun from close range. The cactus rocked back and forth a couple of times before falling on the perpetrator and killing him.

HIGHLIGHTS: A pleasant hike through gorgeous saguaro forest to a saddle on the rugged Tucson Mountains.

TYPE OF TRIP: Out-and-back.

DISTANCE: 3 miles.

DIFFICULTY: Moderate.

PERMITTED USES: Hiking.

MAPS: Saguaro National Park National Geographic.

SPECIAL CONSIDERATIONS: During the hot summer months, plan to hike early in the day and carry plenty of water.

PARKING AND FACILITIES: The trailhead is next to the Ez-Kim-In-Zin Picnic Area, which has parking and restrooms.

FINDING THE TRAILHEAD: From the Red Hills Visitor Center, turn right on Kinney Road. After 2.1 miles turn right onto Sandario Road. In just 0.2 mile, turn right on Golden Gate Road, then drive 3.8 miles to the Sendero Esperanza Trailhead, which is on the right.

This hike takes you across desert flats through fine stands of saguaro cacti. Look for holes in the saguaros, well above the ground, as you walk. Several different birds and animals make their homes by hollowing out these holes. After the cactus dies, falls, and decays, you can sometimes find the intact nests, which are known as saguaro "boots."

The Sendero Esperanza Trail partially follows the route of an old road, as do many trails in the Tucson Mountains. These roads were usually built by miners and prospectors before the creation of the national park. The desert has attracted prospectors since the beginning of European settlement, and prospectors were often the first people to explore a desert area. Prospects are everywhere, usually just small holes in the ground where a prospector explored a likely looking rock outcrop. Some prospect holes are deep enough to be dangerous and are sometimes partially hidden by brush. One giveaway is the heaps of spoil, the dirt and rocks removed from the hole and piled nearby, though sometimes the spoil gets washed away in floods.

After a mile of gradual ascent, the Sendero Esperanza Trail climbs to meet the Hugh Norris Trail on the crest of the Tucson Mountains in a saddle. Views of the surrounding desert hills are great from this saddle, and for even better views, you can hike east on the Hugh Norris Trail, going all the way to Wasson Peak if desired. See the Hugh Norris Trail for information on this section.

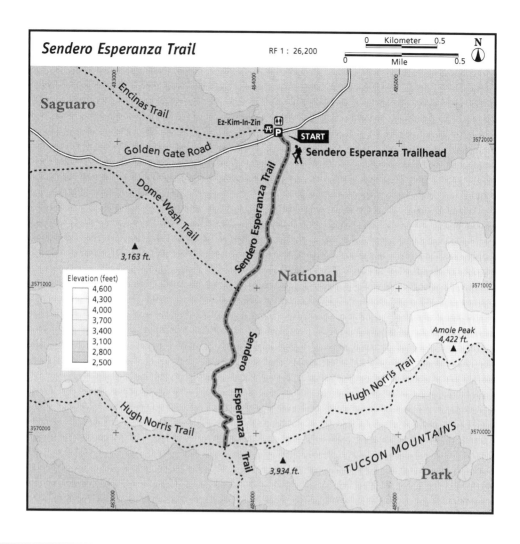

Sendero Esperanza Trail

RF 1 : 26,200

Kilometer 0.5

Mile 0.5

N

Saguaro

Encinas Trail

Ez-Kim-In-Zin

START

Sendero Esperanza Trailhead

Golden Gate Road

Sendero Esperanza Trail

Dome Wash Trail

▲ 3,163 ft.

Elevation (feet)
4,600
4,300
4,000
3,700
3,400
3,100
2,800
2,500

National

Amole Peak
4,422 ft.
▲

Hugh Norris Trail

Sendero

Esperanza

Hugh Norris Trail

Trail

▲ 3,934 ft.

TUCSON MOUNTAINS

Park

Hugh Norris Trail

HIGHLIGHTS: This popular hike follows the main crest of the Tucson Mountains for an exceptionally scenic hike to the highest peak in the range.

TYPE OF TRIP: Out-and-back.

DISTANCE: 7.8 miles.

DIFFICULTY: Moderate.

PERMITTED USES: Hiking.

MAPS: Saguaro National Park National Geographic.

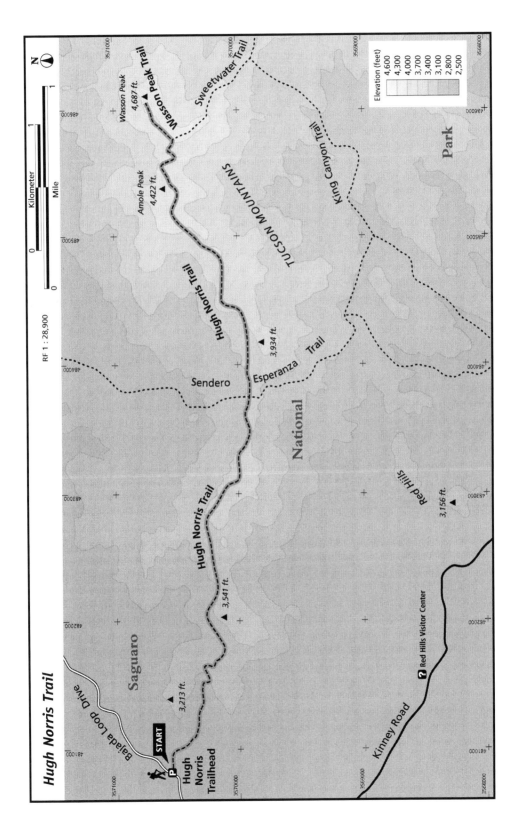

SPECIAL CONSIDERATIONS: During the hot summer months, plan your hike for early in the morning and carry plenty of water. The trail climbs more than 2,000 feet.

PARKING AND FACILITIES: None.

FINDING THE TRAILHEAD: From the Red Hills Visitor Center, turn right and drive northwest 1.7 miles on Kinney Road. Turn right on the Bajada Loop Drive and continue 0.8 mile to the Hugh Norris Trailhead, which is on the right. The trailhead is at the end of the two-way portion of the Hohokam Road scenic loop.

Named for a Tohono O'odham police chief, the Hugh Norris Trail starts from Hohokam Road, which is part of the Bajada Loop Drive, and climbs east up a small, unnamed canyon in the Tucson Mountains. A few switchbacks lead to a saddle, and after passing through another saddle, the trail climbs around the north side of a small peak. The trail soon gains the crest of the main ridge and more or less follows this ridgeline east and down to a saddle, where the Sendero Esperanza Trail crosses. Continue east on the Hugh Norris Trail, which now resumes its steady climb along the ridge. You'll notice that the saguaro cacti start to give way to high desert grassland as you gain elevation, especially on the north-facing slopes. After you pass the south side of Amole Peak, a few steep switchbacks lead back to the main ridge and a trail junction. Here the Sweetwater Trail heads east; turn left (north) on the Wasson Peak Trail and hike 0.2 mile to the summit. Wasson Peak is named for John Wasson, an early editor of the *Tucson Citizen*.

Your effort is rewarded with a 360-degree view of the Tucson Mountains, Avra Valley to the west, Tucson and the Santa Catalina and Rincon Mountains to the east, and in the distant south, the Santa Rita Mountains.

Saguaro cacti are extremely susceptible to subfreezing temperatures, which is why the Sonoran Desert is the only one of the four North American deserts that support them. The Mojave, Great Basin, and Chihuahuan Deserts are all too cold. Even in the Sonoran Desert, the range of the saguaros is limited by the local climate. As you look around, you'll notice that saguaros march further up south- and west-facing slopes than they do on north and east aspects. This is because north and east slopes get less heat from the sun, especially in the winter, and subfreezing temperatures are both more common and more prolonged. Even a slight, short-term shift in the local climate will kill the most exposed, highest stands of saguaros.

On the other hand, as you gain elevation in the Tucson Mountains, the slopes become slightly wetter and not quite as hot as the lower slopes. This causes a transition to the Upper Sonoran life zone, which is just moist enough to allow some grasses to grow.

Wasson Peak, the highest point in the Tucson Mountains

MILES AND DIRECTIONS

0.0 Start at the Hugh Norris Trailhead.

2.2 Cross the Sendero Esperanza Trail.

3.7 Turn left on Wasson Peak Trail.

3.9 Arrive at Wasson Peak.

7.8 Return to the Hugh Norris Trailhead.

King Canyon Trail

HIGHLIGHTS: An alternative route to popular Wasson Peak using the King Canyon and Sweetwater Trails.

TYPE OF TRIP: Out-and-back.

DISTANCE: 6 miles.

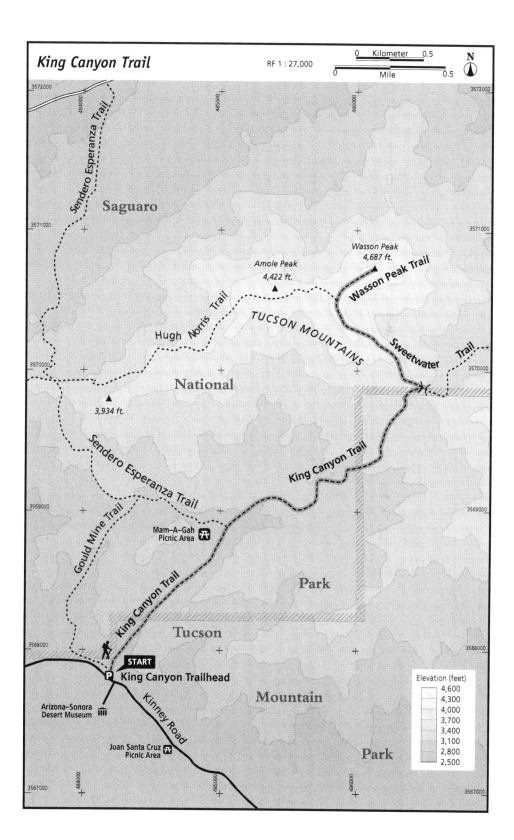

DIFFICULTY: Moderate.

PERMITTED USES: Hiking.

MAPS: Saguaro National Park National Geographic.

SPECIAL CONSIDERATIONS: Carry plenty of water during the hot summer months. This trail climbs 1,700 feet.

PARKING AND FACILITIES: Dirt parking lot without facilities; the walk-in Mam-A-Gah Picnic Area is located 0.9 mile up the King Canyon Trail.

FINDING THE TRAILHEAD: From the Red Hills Visitor Center, turn left (east) on Kinney Road and drive 1.9 miles to the King Canyon/Gould Mine Trailhead, which is a dirt parking lot on the left just before the Arizona–Sonora Desert Museum.

Two trails leave the parking area; head northeast on the King Canyon Trail, an old mining road. You can see elaborate cut stone work that was done during the construction of this road in several places.

Occasionally a prospector actually discovered a valuable mineral deposit. In order to "prove the claim" and eventually acquire ownership of the public land containing the mineral deposit, a prospector had to develop the find and show that the deposit was rich enough to be profitably mined. This usually involved constructing a road, or at least a good trail, to the claim. Luckily for the future national park and wilderness, most mining claims in the Tucson Mountains were unprofitable.

The USGS topographic map of this area shows the Mile Wide Mine on the slopes to the east, and you can see the scars of several old roads built to reach mines on the steep hillsides. Although initial reports in 1916 were optimistic that the mines in the head of King Canyon would be major copper producers, little copper was produced and the mine works were eventually abandoned.

The trail continues up King Canyon and after 0.9 mile passes the Mam-A-Gah Picnic Area and the Sendero Esperanza Trail. Stay right on the King Canyon Trail as it climbs through a Sonoran Desert basin studded with saguaro and cholla cacti. Shortly, the trail begins a steep climb up a ridge. When the King Canyon Trail reaches a saddle on the main crest of the Tucson Mountains, it ends at the Sweetwater Trail. Here, you can look down a canyon to the northeast and see part of the Tucson valley and the Santa Catalina Mountains.

Turn left and follow the Sweetwater Trail up a series of switchbacks that climb the steep ridge to the west. You'll see several marked and fenced old mine shafts next to the trail along this section. About 0.6 mile of this steep ascent leads to the junction of the Hugh Norris and Wasson Peak Trails. Turn right on the Wasson Peak Trail and hike 0.2 mile to the summit.

MILES AND DIRECTIONS

0.0 Start at the King Canyon Trailhead.

0.9 Pass the Sendero Esperanza Trail and Mam-A-Gah Picnic Area; stay right on the King Canyon Trail.

2.2 Turn left on Sweetwater Trail.

2.8 Turn right on the Wasson Peak Trail.

3.0 Arrive at Wasson Peak.

6.0 Return to the King Canyon Trailhead.

Brown Mountain

HIGHLIGHTS: An easy hike in Tucson Mountain Park along the top of a desert ridge with 50-mile views.

TYPE OF TRIP: Out-and-back.

DISTANCE: 2.8 miles.

DIFFICULTY: Easy.

PERMITTED USES: Hiking.

MAPS: Saguaro National Park National Geographic.

SPECIAL CONSIDERATIONS: During the hot summer months, plan to hike early in the day and carry plenty of water.

PARKING AND FACILITIES: Paved parking area without facilities. Restrooms are available at nearby Brown Mountain Picnic Area.

FINDING THE TRAILHEAD: From the Red Hills Visitor Center, turn left on Kinney Road and drive 3.5 miles to the unsigned trailhead on the right. This parking area is past the Arizona–Sonora Desert Museum but just before the Brown Mountain Picnic Area.

Head south toward the east end of Brown Mountain, staying right at two unsigned trail junctions. After the second junction, the trail turns sharply northwest and starts to climb the east slopes of Brown Mountain. As you climb, the views expand. Visible to the southeast, at the foot of the mountain, is the Brown Mountain Picnic Area, and beyond it, Gilbert Ray Campground. Once on the ridge crest, the trail more or less follows the crest northwest. There is a great variety of saguaros along the trail, including a number of young saguaros only about 5 or 6 feet tall.

The Brown Mountain Trail continues to the northwest end of the ridge, which is a good turnaround point. (From here, the trail descends to the Juan

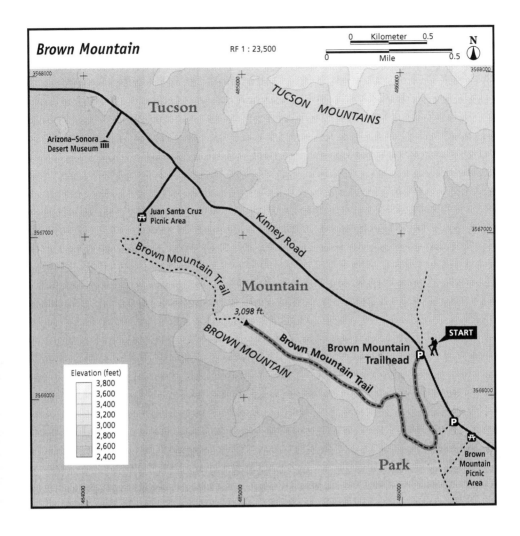

RF 1 : 23,500

Kilometer

Mile

N

Tucson

TUCSON MOUNTAINS

Arizona–Sonora
Desert Museum

Juan Santa Cruz
Picnic Area

Brown Mountain Trail

Kinney Road

Mountain

3,098 ft.

BROWN MOUNTAIN

Brown Mountain Trail

Brown Mountain
Trailhead

START

Elevation (feet)

| 3,800 |
| 3,600 |
| 3,400 |
| 3,200 |
| 3,000 |
| 2,800 |
| 2,600 |
| 2,400 |

Park

Brown
Mountain
Picnic
Area

Santa Cruz Picnic Area.) Brown Mountain is a detached, outlying ridge and gives you a panoramic view of the Tucson Mountains, as well as the sweep of Avra Valley to the west and the Baboquivari Mountains to the southwest. The Baboquivari Mountains are marked by two prominent and unmistakable summits. Monolithic Baboquivari Peak, toward the south end of the range, is one of the few Arizona summits that requires rock-climbing skills and equipment. Kitt Peak, at the north end of the range, is the site of a large solar and stellar observatory. The telescope domes are easily spotted from more than 30 miles away.

North of the turnaround point, partly blocked by the northwestern end of Brown Mountain, you can see the Arizona–Sonora Desert Museum, a place

Brown Mountain Trail and a young saguaro, Tucson Mountains

worth visiting if you wish to learn more about the plants and animals of the Sonoran Desert. See the Tucson chapter for information on the museum.

Brown Mountain is named for Cornelius Brown, who helped create Tucson Mountain Park in 1929 and is regarded as the father of the park.

MILES AND DIRECTIONS

0.0 Begin at the trailhead.

0.3 Stay right at the unsigned trail junction.

0.4 Again, stay right at this unsigned trail junction.

1.4 Arrive at the turnaround point at the northwest end of Brown Mountain.

2.8 Return to the trailhead.

Yetman Trail

HIGHLIGHTS: The David Yetman Trail passes through varied Sonoran Desert terrain at the southern end of the Tucson Mountains in Tucson Mountain Park. It can be done as an out-and-back hike or one-way with a car shuttle.

TYPE OF TRIP: Out-and-back or one-way.

DISTANCE: 11.6 miles out-and-back.

DIFFICULTY: Moderate.

PERMITTED USES: Hiking, horseback riding, mountain biking.

MAPS: Saguaro National Park National Geographic.

SPECIAL CONSIDERATIONS: During the hot summer months, plan to hike early in the day and carry plenty of water.

PARKING AND FACILITIES: Yetman Trailhead (West) is paved; David Yetman Trailhead (East) is reached via a dirt road.

FINDING THE TRAILHEAD: From the Red Hills Visitor Center, turn left (east) on Kinney Road. Drive 4.7 miles, then turn left on Gates Pass Road. Drive another 1.7 miles, then turn right into the Yetman Trailhead (West). To reach the Yetman Trailhead East, turn right on Gates Pass Road. After 2.9 miles, turn right on Caminino del Oeste and drive 0.9 mile south to the end of the road.

This hike can be done as an out-and-back or as a one-way hike with a car shuttle by dropping a second vehicle at Yetman Trailhead (East). Starting from the

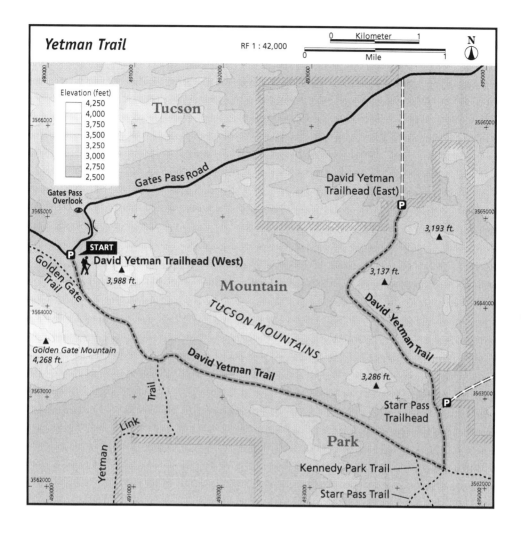

Yetman Trail

RF 1 : 42,000

Elevation (feet)
4,250
4,000
3,750
3,500
3,250
3,000
2,750
2,500

Tucson

Gates Pass Road

Gates Pass
Overlook

David Yetman
Trailhead (East)

3,193 ft.

START

David Yetman Trailhead (West)

3,988 ft.

Mountain

3,137 ft.

Golden Gate Trail

Golden Gate Mountain
4,268 ft.

TUCSON MOUNTAINS

David Yetman Trail

David Yetman Trail

3,286 ft.

Trail

Link

Starr Pass
Trailhead

Park

Yetman

Kennedy Park Trail

Starr Pass Trail

west trailhead, the David Yetman Trail heads southeast toward a pass. At the pass the Golden Gate Trail merges from the right; stay left and follow the Yetman Trail down to the flats at the base of Golden Gate Mountain. Here the Yetman Link Trail forks right; stay left on the Yetman Trail and follow it east. Climbing into the Tucson Mountains once again, the Yetman Trail crosses another unnamed pass and then descends a canyon to the east. After emerging into a broad desert basin, the Yetman Trail meets the Kennedy Park Trail; stay left on the Yetman Trail. Stay left at the junction with the Starr Pass Trail also, and follow the Yetman Trail north past the Starr Pass (east) Trailhead and over a low pass. Now the Yetman Trail descends generally north, following a drainage system the remaining distance to Yetman Trailhead (East). This is the end of the hike if you left a shuttle vehicle here; otherwise, return the way you came.

The trail was named after David Yetman, who served on the Pima County Board of Supervisors from 1977 to 1988. Yetman was a strong defender of the environment, and the trail was named to honor him after his retirement.

MILES AND DIRECTIONS

0.0 Begin at the David Yetman Trailhead (West).

0.4 Stay left at the Golden Gate Trail.

1.1 Stay left at the Yetman Link Trail.

3.1 Stay left at the Kennedy Park Trail.

3.3 Stay left at the Starr Pass Trail.

3.8 Stay left at the Starr Pass (east) Trailhead.

5.8 Arrive at the David Yetman Trailhead (East).

11.6 Return to the trailhead.

Saguaro National Park East

Also known as the Rincon Mountain District, the eastern division of Saguaro National Park lies at the east edge of Tucson, is the larger of the two divisions, and includes most of the Rincon Mountains. The small portion of the Rincons not in the park is part of the Coronado National Forest. Most of the park and much of the national forest portion of the Rincons are in the Saguaro and Rincon Mountain Wilderness Areas. This "Sky Island" range varies from 2,800 feet at the desert floor to 8,664 feet at Mica Mountain and encompasses four distinct life zones along the rise, from desert scrub to fir forest. An extensive trail system covers the foothills and reaches to the summits. Unlike the Santa Catalina Mountains, there is no road to the top, and the trails are long, making the high country the domain of the backpacker, the horseman, and only the most ambitious of day hikers.

The Rincon Mountains form a sort of inverted L. A long ridge, Tanque Verde Ridge, rises from the Rincon Visitor Center area and ascends steadily east to culminate in the mountains' summit, Mica Mountain. From Mica Mountain, Heartbreak Ridge runs generally south, dipping to Happy Valley Saddle before rising to the range's second-highest peak, Rincon Peak.

Getting to the Park

Tucson is served by scheduled airline and bus service and is traversed by Interstate 10. Once in Tucson, you'll need a car to explore the parks and the Santa

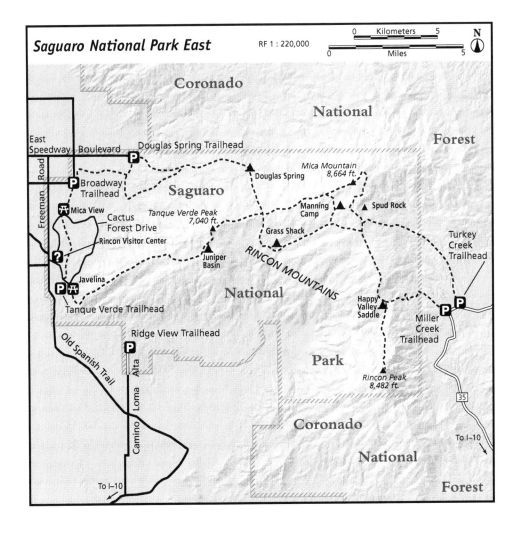

Coronado

National

Forest

East
Speedway Boulevard   Douglas Spring Trailhead

Freeman Road

Broadway
Trailhead

Saguaro

Mica Mountain
8,664 ft.

Douglas Spring

Mica View

Cactus
Forest Drive

Tanque Verde Peak
7,040 ft.

Manning
Camp

Spud Rock

Rincon Visitor Center

Grass Shack

Juniper
Basin

RINCON MOUNTAINS

Turkey
Creek
Trailhead

Javelina

National

Happy
Valley
Saddle

Tanque Verde Trailhead

Miller
Creek
Trailhead

Ridge View Trailhead

Park

Old Spanish Trail

Camino Loma Alta

Rincon Peak
8,482 ft.

35

Coronado

To I–10

To I–10

National

Forest

Catalina Mountains. From I–10, you can reach Saguaro National Park East from the west or the south. The following directions take you to the Rincon Visitor Center as a starting point for further exploration.

From central Tucson, head east on Broadway Road to Houghton Road and turn right. Drive south 2.7 miles and then turn left on Old Spanish Trail. Continue southeast 2.8 miles to the park and the Rincon Visitor Center turnoff, on the left.

From I–10 north, exit at Valencia Road, turn left, and drive 3 miles to Kolb Road. Turn left, go 1.7 miles, and then turn right on Irvington Road. After 4 miles, turn left on Houghton Road, drive 1 mile, turn right on Escalante Road, and drive 2 miles to Old Spanish Trail. Turn left, then, after 0.2 mile, turn right at the park and Rincon Visitor Center turnoff.

From I–10 south, exit at Houghton Road and head north 7.9 miles to Escalante Road. Turn right and drive 2 miles to Old Spanish Trail. Turn left, drive 0.2 mile, and then turn right at the park and Rincon Visitor Center turnoff.

Getting around the Park

Starting from the Rincon Visitor Center, Cactus Forest Drive is a one-way scenic drive through the Sonoran Desert foothills. This road also accesses several trailheads, viewpoints, and picnic areas. Freeman Road runs along the west border of the park, and Speedway Boulevard along the northwest border. Access to the south and east sides of the park is via dirt roads only and is mainly of interest to the hiker and equestrian. These approaches are described in the "Trails" section later in the chapter.

Finding the Trailheads

Many of the trailheads in Saguaro National Park East start near the Rincon Visitor Center and are accessible from paved roads. As with the other visitor centers, the Rincon Visitor Center is a perfect place to get familiar with the Rincon Mountains, so I use it as the starting point for all trailheads in the east portion of the park, including the few trailheads on the south and east sides of the park that are accessible only via graded dirt roads.

Visitor Centers and Amenities

The Rincon Visitor Center, at the park entrance next to Old Spanish Trail, is the best place to become familiar with Saguaro National Park East. The visitor center has exhibits that explain the natural history of the Sonoran Desert and the Rincon Mountains, as well as programs and interpretive walks.

Several picnic areas are located along Cactus Forest Drive. Since the park is adjacent to Tucson, just about every amenity you could want is close by, including motels, hotels, bed-and-breakfast inns, and resorts.

Campgrounds

There are no auto campgrounds within Saguaro National Park East. The Santa Catalina Mountains have a number of developed campgrounds that are accessible from the Catalina Highway. See the "Santa Catalina Mountains" section for details.

Backcountry camping is allowed at designated sites in the Rincon Mountains. A permit is required and is available at the Rincon Visitor Center.

Mica Mountain is the high point in the Rincon high country, viewed here from Happy Valley Lookout.

Scenic Drive

Cactus Forest Loop Drive

HIGHLIGHTS: This scenic drive provides access to the short Desert Ecology Nature Trail and several picnic areas, plus views of saguaro cacti and the Rincon Mountains.

TYPE OF TRIP: Loop.

DISTANCE: 6 miles.

Starting from the Rincon Visitor Center, the Cactus Forest Loop Drive winds for about 6 miles through a classic section of the Sonoran Desert Valley, with large stands of saguaro cacti as well as expansive views of the Rincon Mountains. The entire loop is paved and most of it is one-way. In the summer, plan your drive for the cool of early morning. Take a picnic and plan to have lunch at one of the picnic areas, and take a walk along the very short Desert Ecology Nature Trail or a short distance along one of the other trails.

From the Rincon Visitor Center, stay left on Cactus Forest Drive to enter the one-way loop. There are pull-outs and scenic overlooks all along the drive. At the north end of the loop, you'll pass the short spur road to Mica View Picnic Area and Trailhead and then the Desert Ecology Trail. The road now heads east and then turns south along the base of Tanque Verde Ridge. The Tanque Verde and Freeman Homestead Trailheads are near the Javelina Picnic Area at the south end of the loop drive. Here the road turns northwest and becomes two-way for the return to the Rincon Visitor Center.

Trails

Garwood Trail

HIGHLIGHTS: An easy walk through Sonoran Desert foothills to an old dam site.

TYPE OF TRIP: Out-and-back.

DISTANCE: 3.6 miles.

DIFFICULTY: Easy.

PERMITTED USES: Hiking, horseback riding.

MAPS: Saguaro National Park National Geographic.

SPECIAL CONSIDERATIONS: During the hot summer months, plan to hike early in the day and carry plenty of water.

PARKING AND FACILITIES: Dirt parking area without facilities.

FINDING THE TRAILHEAD: From the Rincon Visitor Center, turn right on Old Spanish Trail, which becomes North Freeman Road. Continue 3.6 miles and then turn right on East Speedway Boulevard. Continue 3 miles east to the end of the road at the Douglas Spring Trailhead.

From the Douglas Spring Trailhead, follow the Douglas Spring Trail east across the desert flats 0.3 mile, then turn right on the Garwood Trail. There are numerous side trails that cross and intersect, but stay on the Garwood Trail to its end and then turn left on the Carrillo Trail. Follow the Carrillo Trail up a hill and along the side of a small canyon to Garwood Dam. Look for pools of water in the canyon below the dam, which often persist through the dry season.

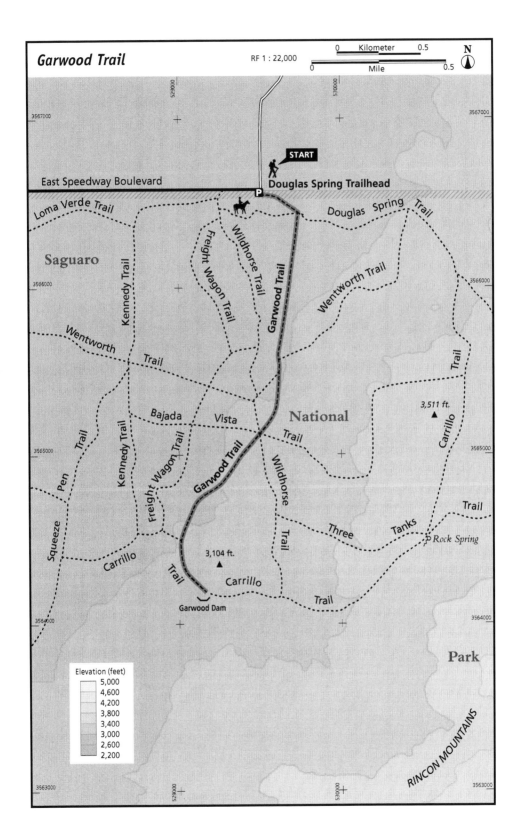

Garwood Trail

RF 1 : 22,000

Kilometer 0 — 0.5
Mile 0 — 0.5

N

START

Douglas Spring Trailhead

East Speedway Boulevard

Loma Verde Trail

Saguaro

Kennedy Trail

Freight Wagon Trail

Wildhorse Trail

Garwood Trail

Douglas Spring Trail

Wentworth Trail

Wentworth Trail

Trail

3,511 ft. ▲

Carrillo Trail

Bajada

Vista

National

Trail

Pen Trail

Kennedy Trail

Freight Wagon Trail

Garwood Trail

Wildhorse Trail

Trail

Three Tanks

Rock Spring

Trail

Squeeze

Carrillo

Trail

3,104 ft. ▲

Carrillo

Trail

Garwood Dam

Park

Elevation (feet)
5,000
4,600
4,200
3,800
3,400
3,000
2,600
2,200

RINCON MOUNTAINS

3567000
3566000
3565000
3564000
3563000

Garwood Dam, Rincon Mountains

An ability to spot small water pockets like these is one of the skills that experienced desert hikers, and especially backpackers, soon develop.

Garwood Dam is the goal for the hike, at a point offering views of the Rincon Mountain foothills as well as the desert plain at their foot. The now abandoned concrete dam was originally built across Wildhorse Canyon to supply water for a homestead. Notice how the saguaro cacti and scrub of the Lower Sonoran life zone give way to the grasslands of the Upper Sonoran life zone not too far above you.

MILES AND DIRECTIONS

0.0 Start at the Douglas Spring Trailhead.

0.3 Turn right at the Garwood Trail.

0.6 Stay right at the Wentworth Trail.

0.7 Stay left at the Wentworth Trail.

1.1 The Bajada Vista and Wildhorse Trails cross; go straight ahead on Garwood Trail.

1.6 The Garwood Trail ends at Carrillo Trail; turn left.

1.8 Arrive at Garwood Dam.

3.6 Return to the trailhead.

Bridal Wreath Falls

HIGHLIGHTS: Using the Douglas Spring Trail, this hike takes you to a seasonal waterfall in the foothills of the Rincon Mountains.

TYPE OF TRIP: Out-and-back.

DISTANCE: 5.2 miles.

DIFFICULTY: Moderate.

PERMITTED USES: Hiking, horseback riding.

MAPS: Saguaro National Park National Geographic.

SPECIAL CONSIDERATIONS: Carry plenty of water during the hot summer months.

PARKING AND FACILITIES: Dirt parking area without facilities.

FINDING THE TRAILHEAD: From the Rincon Visitor Center, turn right on Old Spanish Trail, which becomes North Freeman Road. Continue 3.6 miles and turn right on East Speedway Boulevard. Continue 3 miles east to the end of the road at the Douglas Spring Trailhead.

From the Douglas Spring Trailhead, hike east on the Douglas Spring Trail across the Sonoran Desert plain. Numerous trails branch right in this section; stay left on the Douglas Spring Trail at all of them. The easy section ends as the trail turns southeast and begins climbing a ridge in the foothills of the Rincon Mountains. Look back frequently for good views of the Tucson valley, and to the northwest, the Santa Catalina Mountains.

Eventually the trail drops into a ravine and turns back to the east. As the trail emerges onto a flat, you'll notice that the route has climbed into the Upper Sonoran life zone. The saguaros are gone, replaced by the high desert grassland characteristic of this life zone.

In 1989 lightning started a wildfire that eventually burned a large area on the north slopes of Tanque Verde Ridge, including the upper portion of the Douglas Spring Trail. Evidence of the fire is visible in the form of blackened brush and bits of charcoal, but it is remarkable how fast the landscape recovers from a wildfire.

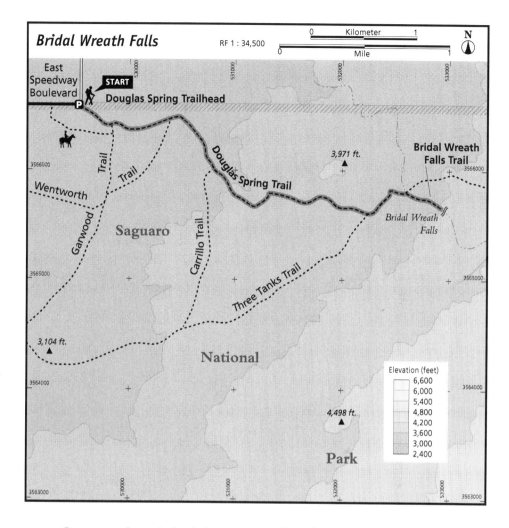

Cottonwoods mark the drainage just south of the trail, where seasonal water sometimes surfaces. Just after passing the Three Tanks Trail, turn right on the Bridal Wreath Falls Trail, which goes south 0.4 mile into a small canyon. The falls are seasonal, and the best chances to see them running are after snowmelt in March and April or after a thunderstorm during late summer.

MILES AND DIRECTIONS

0.0 Start at the Douglas Spring Trailhead.

0.3 Turn left at the Garwood Trail.

0.5 Stay left at the Wentworth Trail.

0.9 Stay left at the Carrillo Trail.

2.1 Stay left at the Three Tanks Trail.

2.2 Turn right at the Bridal Wreath Falls Trail.

2.6 Arrive at Bridal Wreath Falls.

5.2 Return to the trailhead.

Cactus Forest Trail

HIGHLIGHTS: This trail starts from the scenic loop drive and wanders north through gentle desert terrain past magnificent stands of saguaro cacti. The first portion of the trail, inside the scenic loop drive, is open to mountain bikers.

TYPE OF TRIP: Out-and-back or one-way (cyclists can optionally return on the paved loop drive).

DISTANCE: 8.4 miles.

DIFFICULTY: Moderate.

PERMITTED USES: Hiking; cycling on the southern section of the trail inside the scenic loop drive.

MAPS: Saguaro National Park National Geographic.

SPECIAL CONSIDERATIONS: Carry plenty of water during the hot summer months.

PARKING AND FACILITIES: None.

FINDING THE TRAILHEAD: From the Rincon Visitor Center, turn right on Cactus Forest Drive and go 0.9 mile to the Cactus Forest Trailhead South on the left. To reach the Cactus Forest Trailhead North from the Rincon Visitor Center, turn left on Cactus Forest Drive and go 2.7 miles to the trailhead, which is on the left. To reach the Broadway Trailhead from the Rincon Visitor Center, turn right on Old Spanish Trail, which becomes North Freeman Road. Continue 2.6 miles, then turn right on East Broadway Boulevard. Drive 0.7 mile to the Broadway Trailhead, on the right.

You can hike this trail as an out-and-back, or leave a vehicle at the Cactus Forest Trailhead North for a one-way hike of 2.4 miles. Or you can leave a vehicle at the Broadway Trailhead for a one-way hike of 4.2 miles.

Mountain bikers are allowed on the first portion of the trail, within the Cactus Forest Loop Drive. When you reach the Cactus Forest Trailhead North, you have the options of returning on the trail the way you came or turning right on the one-way Cactus Forest Loop Drive and following it back to the Cactus Forest Trailhead South, a distance of 4.2 miles on the paved road.

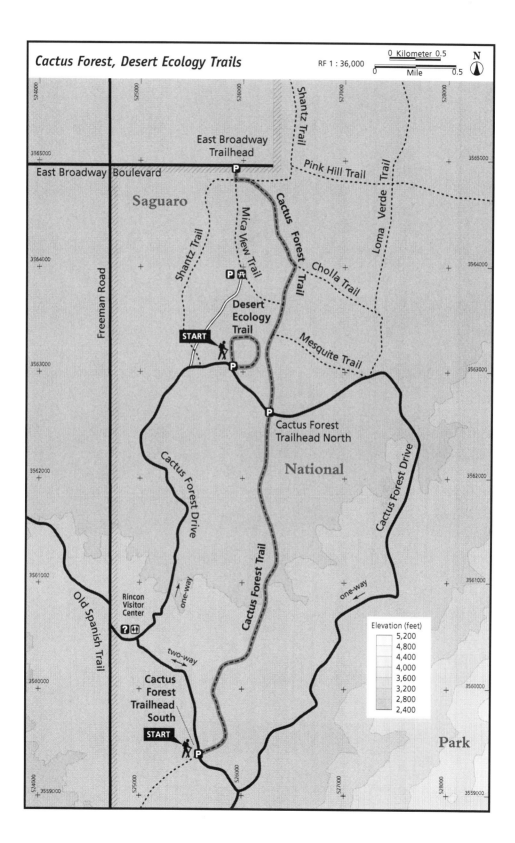

Cactus Forest, Desert Ecology Trails

RF 1 : 36,000

0 Kilometer 0.5
0 Mile 0.5

N

East Broadway Trailhead

Shantz Trail

Pink Hill Trail

Saguaro

East Broadway Boulevard

Freeman Road

Shantz Trail

Mica View Trail

Cactus Forest Trail

Loma Verde Trail

Cholla Trail

Desert Ecology Trail

START

Mesquite Trail

Cactus Forest Trailhead North

National

Cactus Forest Drive

Cactus Forest Drive

one-way

Cactus Forest Trail

Rincon Visitor Center

two-way

Cactus Forest Trailhead South

START

Old Spanish Trail

Elevation (feet)
5,200
4,800
4,400
4,000
3,600
3,200
2,800
2,400

Park

Prickly pear and ocotillo, common plants of the Sonoran Desert, Rincon Mountains foothills

From the Cactus Forest Trailhead South, the Cactus Forest Trail wanders generally north through the gentle desert plain, winding through stands of tall saguaro cacti. If you left a shuttle vehicle at the Cactus Forest Trailhead North, you'll have to complete the one-way loop drive by turning right.

The Cactus Forest Trail continues north across the road, and the Mesquite Trail soon comes in from the right. Stay left to the junction with the Mica View Trail, where you should stay right on the Cactus Forest Trail. At yet another junction, the Cholla Trail comes in from the right; stay left and follow the Cactus Forest Trail to the Shantz Trail, where you'll turn left and walk just 0.1 mile farther to the East Broadway Trailhead. This is the end of the hike if you left a shuttle vehicle here; otherwise, return the way you came.

Heavy cattle grazing took place in the western foothills of the Rincon Mountains for many years, which had a severe impact on the saguaro cacti. Cattle destroyed the nurse trees on which young saguaros depend for survival and also trampled the saguaros themselves. As a result, the area of the Cactus Forest Trail is populated mostly with old saguaros.

MILES AND DIRECTIONS

0.0 Begin at the Cactus Forest Trailhead South.

2.4 Reach the Cactus Forest Trailhead North.

2.9 Stay left at the Mesquite Trail.

3.2 Stay right at the Mica View Trail.

3.4 Stay left at the Cholla Trail.

4.0 Turn left at the Shantz Trail.

4.1 Arrive at the East Broadway Trailhead.

8.4 Return to the Cactus Forest Trailhead South if you'd like to make this a round-trip.

Desert Ecology Trail

See map on page 89.

HIGHLIGHTS: A paved, wheelchair-accessible interpretive trail with signs explaining how desert plants and animals deal with the arid desert.

TYPE OF TRIP: Loop.

DISTANCE: 0.7 mile.

DIFFICULTY: Easy.

PERMITTED USES: Hiking.

MAPS: Saguaro National Park National Geographic.

SPECIAL CONSIDERATIONS: None.

PARKING AND FACILITIES: Parking is available, but there are no facilities at the trailhead. The trail is paved and wheelchair accessible.

FINDING THE TRAILHEAD: From the Rincon Visitor Center, turn left on Cactus Forest Drive and go 2.3 miles to the Desert Ecology Trailhead. Because the road is one-way, after the hike you'll have to finish the 6.1 miles of the loop drive back to the Rincon Visitor Center. This would be a good hike to do along with the longer Freeman Homestead Nature Trail on a drive of the loop.

The Desert Ecology Trail is an interpretive nature trail that is fitted with signs along the way that explain the fascinating ways in which the plants and animals of the Sonoran Desert interact and depend on one another. One such animal/plant relationship exists between yuccas and moths, a relationship that is invisible to the casual observer. Each species of yucca depends on a single species of moth to pollinate it. Both are dependent on each other—without the yucca, the moth would die out, and without the moth, that species of yucca would vanish.

Prickly pear cactus is the most common cactus in the Sonoran Desert.

Freeman Homestead Nature Trail

HIGHLIGHTS: This nature trail explores the homesteading period in what is now Saguaro National Park.

TYPE OF TRIP: Lollipop.

DISTANCE: 1.1 miles.

DIFFICULTY: Easy.

PERMITTED USES: Hiking.

MAPS: Saguaro National Park National Geographic.

SPECIAL CONSIDERATIONS: None.

PARKING AND FACILITIES: There are no facilities at the trailhead, but the wheelchair-accessible Javelina Picnic Area is nearby.

FINDING THE TRAILHEAD: From the Rincon Visitor Center, turn right on Cactus Forest Drive and drive 1.2 miles to the Javelina Picnic Area turnoff. Turn right and go 0.2 mile to the Freeman Homestead Trailhead on the right.

The Freeman Homestead Nature Trail loops through the Sonoran Desert southwest of the Javelina Picnic Area, passing through a fine section of saguaro "forest" and along a wash lined with the ubiquitous mesquite. Interpretive signs describe Tucson's history as well as the challenges of homesteading in the desert.

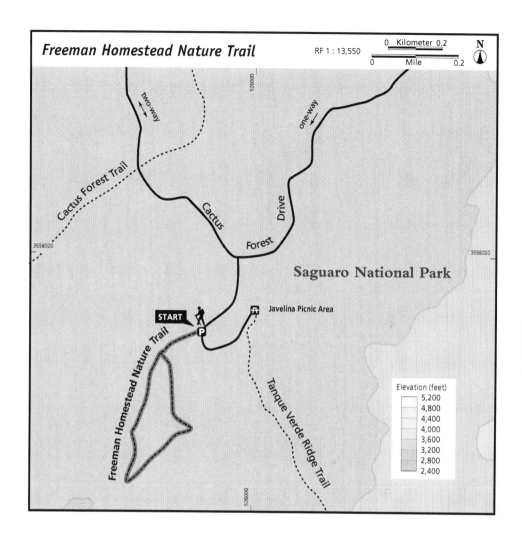

Freeman Homestead Nature Trail

RF 1 : 13,550

Saguaro National Park

Javelina Picnic Area

START

Cactus Forest Trail

Cactus Forest Drive

two-way

one-way

Freeman Homestead Nature Trail

Tanque Verde Ridge Trail

Elevation (feet)
- 5,200
- 4,800
- 4,400
- 4,000
- 3,600
- 3,200
- 2,800
- 2,400

Tanque Verde Ridge Trail

HIGHLIGHTS: A long day hike or overnight hike up Tanque Verde Ridge, the scenic spine of the Rincon Mountains, to Tanque Verde Peak.

TYPE OF TRIP: Out-and-back.

DISTANCE: 15 miles.

DIFFICULTY: Difficult.

PERMITTED USES: Hiking, horseback riding.

MAPS: Saguaro National Park National Geographic.

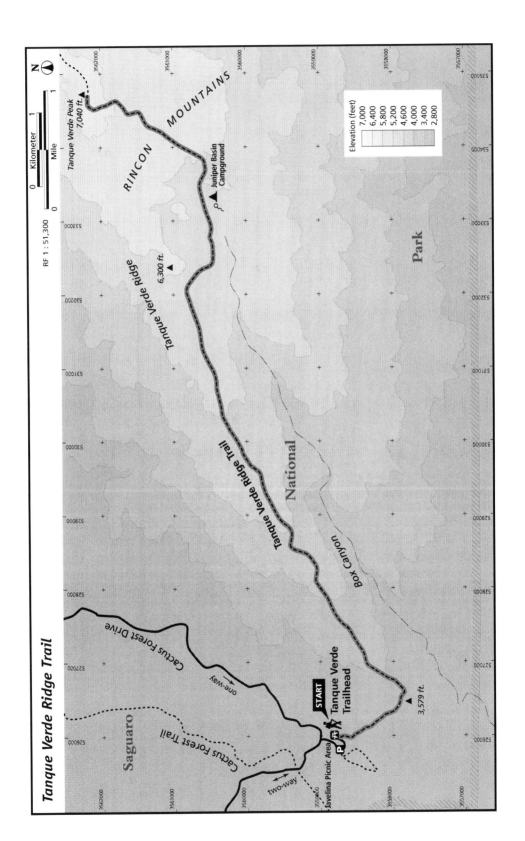

SPECIAL CONSIDERATIONS: Backpackers must have a camping permit, available for a fee from the Rincon Visitor Center in person or by mail (see appendix A for address). On this hike, camping is allowed only at Juniper Basin Campground, where there is a seasonal spring. Don't rely on this spring; carry plenty of water, especially during the hot summer months.

PARKING AND FACILITIES: The trailhead is located at the wheelchair-accessible Javelina Picnic Area, which has paved parking and restrooms.

FINDING THE TRAILHEAD: From the Rincon Visitor Center, turn right on Cactus Forest Drive and drive 1.2 miles to the Javelina Picnic Area turnoff. Turn right and go 0.3 mile to the Tanque Verde Trailhead at the picnic area.

After crossing a drainage, the Tanque Verde Ridge Trail heads southeast and climbs gradually. Almost immediately you'll start to get good views of the Tucson area to the west. Less than a mile from the trailhead, the trail gains the crest of Tanque Verde Ridge and turns to the east. For the next several miles, the trail stays more or less on top of the broad ridge. Views open up as the trail ascends the ridge, and soon include most of the mountains surrounding Tucson. The bulk of the Santa Catalinas rise to the northwest, while the lower Tucson Mountains are at the west side of the Tucson Valley and the Santa Cruz River bed. Beyond the Tucson Mountains you should be able to spot Kitt Peak and the Baboquivari Mountains on a clear day. The sharp peak of Mount Wrightson, the high point of the Santa Rita Mountains, rises to the southwest, and closer at hand, to the southeast, Rincon Peak marks the southern end of the Rincon Mountains.

As you climb you'll gradually leave behind the lower Sonoran Desert and the domain of the saguaro cactus. Saguaros can't stand prolonged subfreezing temperatures, so they disappear from colder north-facing slopes first. Eventually high desert grassland takes over as you continue the steady ascent. At about the 5,000-foot level, a mix of chaparral brush and pinyon-juniper woodland begins to dominate.

As the trail climbs above 5,400 feet, Tanque Verde Ridge becomes broader and less defined, and soon the trail veers southeast away from the ridge crest and contours into the drainages at the head of Box Canyon. Resuming a gradual climb, the Tanque Verde Ridge Trail enters Juniper Basin, which has a seasonal spring and a designated campsite for backpackers.

Above Juniper Basin, the Tanque Verde Ridge Trail turns northeast and climbs back to the crest of Tanque Verde Ridge at Tanque Verde Peak. This 7,040-foot peak is the goal of this hike, but backpackers with more time can explore the extensive trail system in the high country to the east. See the Mica Mountain hike for more information.

MILES AND DIRECTIONS

0.0 Start at the Tanque Verde Trailhead.

5.6 Pass through the Juniper Basin Campground.

7.5 Arrive at Tanque Verde Peak.

15.0 Return to the trailhead.

Ridge View Trail

HIGHLIGHTS: An easy walk to a viewpoint overlooking the rugged south slopes of Tanque Verde Ridge.

TYPE OF TRIP: Out-and-back.

DISTANCE: 1.8 miles.

DIFFICULTY: Easy.

The easy Ridge View Trail wanders through the southern foothills of the Rincon Mountains.

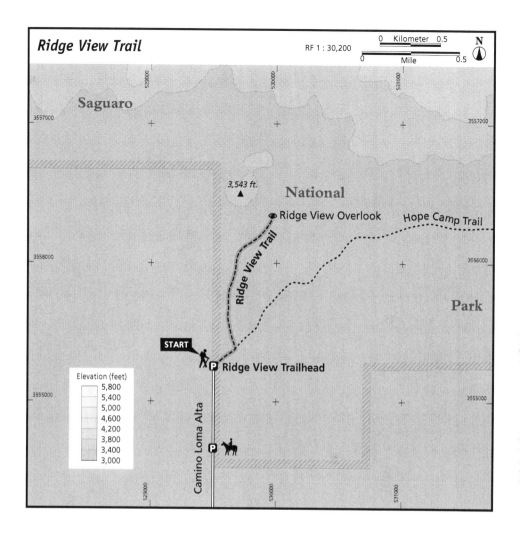

Ridge View Trail

RF 1 : 30,200

Saguaro

National

Ridge View Overlook

Hope Camp Trail

Park

3,543 ft.

Ridge View Trail

START

Ridge View Trailhead

Camino Loma Alta

Elevation (feet)
| 5,800 |
| 5,400 |
| 5,000 |
| 4,600 |
| 4,200 |
| 3,800 |
| 3,400 |
| 3,000 |

PERMITTED USES: Hiking, horseback riding.

MAPS: Saguaro National Park National Geographic.

SPECIAL CONSIDERATIONS: Carry plenty of water during the hot summer months.

PARKING AND FACILITIES: Dirt parking area; no facilities.

FINDING THE TRAILHEAD: From the Rincon Visitor Center, turn left on Old Spanish Trail. Continue 7.2 miles and then turn left on Camino Loma Alta Road. Drive 2.4 miles north to the end of the road.

This easy hike in the Sonoran Desert foothills starts on the Hope Camp Trail, which is popular with horseback riders. After just 0.1 mile you'll turn left on the

Ridge View Trail. The trail follows a dry wash with limited views for 0.8 mile but then abruptly ends on a ridge with good views of the vast sweep of Tanque Verde Ridge. The ridge climbs from the low desert to the northwest to the pine-and-fir forest of the Rincon high country around Mica Mountain and Rincon Peak.

MILES AND DIRECTIONS

0.0 Begin at the Ridge View Trailhead.

0.1 Turn left on Ridge View Trail.

0.9 Arrive at the overlook.

1.8 Return to the trailhead.

Mica Mountain

HIGHLIGHTS: A backpack trip over the summit of the Rincon Mountains via two branches of the Arizona Trail.

TYPE OF TRIP: Loop.

DISTANCE: 20.2 miles.

DIFFICULTY: Difficult.

PERMITTED USES: Hiking; horseback riding (except on the upper Miller Creek Trail, which is closed to stock).

MAPS: Saguaro National Park National Geographic.

SPECIAL CONSIDERATIONS: All the springs on this route are seasonal except Manning Camp Spring, and they dry up during the summer and fall dry seasons. Check with the Rincon Visitor Center before your trip to get the latest information on the springs and other water sources. Spring, after snowmelt, is a good time to do this trip as there will normally be plenty of water sources.

PARKING AND FACILITIES: Dirt parking area; no facilities.

FINDING THE TRAILHEAD: From the Rincon Visitor Center, turn left onto Old Spanish Trail, drive 0.2 mile, then turn right (west) on Escalante Road. Continue 2 miles, then turn left on Houghton Road. Drive south 8.1 miles, then turn left onto Interstate 10 via the I–10 East ramp. After 21.4 miles on I–10, exit at Mescal Road/J-Six Ranch and then turn left on Mescal Road. Initially paved, Mescal Road becomes graded dirt and is marked Forest Road 35. Except after a storm, the road is passable to passenger cars if driven with care. About 15.4 miles from I–10, turn left into the signed Miller Creek Trailhead.

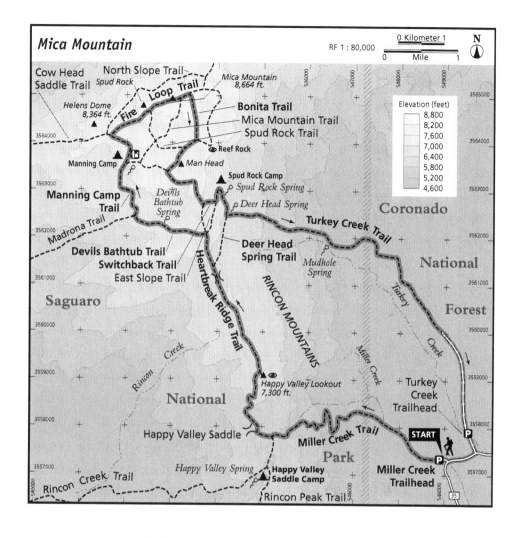

RF 1 : 80,000

0 Kilometer 1

0   Mile   1

N

Cow Head
Saddle Trail

North Slope Trail
Spud Rock

Mica Mountain
8,664 ft.

Helens Dome
8,364 ft.

Fire

Loop Trail

Bonita Trail
Mica Mountain Trail
Spud Rock Trail

Elevation (feet)
8,800
8,200
7,600
7,000
6,400
5,800
5,200
4,600

Reef Rock

Manning Camp

Man Head

Spud Rock Camp
Spud Rock Spring

Manning Camp
Trail

Devils
Bathtub
Spring

Deer Head Spring

Coronado

Madrona Trail

Devils Bathtub Trail
Switchback Trail
East Slope Trail

Deer Head
Spring Trail

Turkey Creek Trail

Mudhole
Spring

National

Saguaro

Heartbreak Ridge Trail

RINCON MOUNTAINS

Turkey

Creek

Forest

Rincon

Creek

Miller Creek

Happy Valley Lookout
7,300 ft.

National

Turkey
Creek
Trailhead

Happy Valley Saddle

Miller Creek Trail

START

P

Park

Rincon Creek Trail

Happy Valley Spring

Happy Valley
Saddle Camp

Rincon Peak Trail

Miller Creek
Trailhead

P

35

From the trailhead, the Miller Creek Trail (the route of the Utah-to-Mexico Arizona Trail) follows Miller Creek, a seasonal stream, west through the oak woodland in the Rincon Mountains foothills. After passing the Saguaro National Park boundary, the trail starts to climb the steep eastern slopes of the Rincon Mountains in a series of broad switchbacks. The trail is rocky and steep in places as it works its way through complex terrain with granite cliffs, large boulders, and chaparral brush. Pinyon pines and junipers start to appear as you climb, and the view of the wild country to the east expands. After the trail swings into a nameless canyon and climbs along a north-facing slope, you'll encounter a few ponderosa pines. The canyon bottom sometimes has water, especially in the spring. When the trail reaches the ridge crest, it meets the Heartbreak Ridge Trail south of Happy Valley Saddle. Happy Valley Camp-

Miller Creek Trail, Rincon Mountains

ground and its seasonal spring are 0.4 mile south on the Rincon Peak Trail. This is the first of several designated campgrounds on or near the loop.

Turn right on the Heartbreak Ridge Trail, which passes near but not actually through Happy Valley Saddle. The area of the saddle has scattered ponderosa pines and heavy chaparral underbrush, but the brush thins as the trail starts the climb northward along the main ridge connecting Rincon Peak to Happy Valley Lookout. Some serious trail work has been done along this section, using cut stone blocks. You'll get good views south toward Happy Valley Saddle and Rincon Peak as the trail climbs. Finally, the Heartbreak Ridge Trail tops out at a junction just north of Happy Valley Lookout. The view from the summit is worth the 0.2-mile walk south on the spur trail to the old fire lookout.

From the junction, continue north on the Heartbreak Ridge Trail, which works its way along the ridge crest with short climbs and descents. More ponderosa pine appear, and there are several nice pine glades. At the north end of the ridge, you'll meet the Deer Head Spring Trail; stay left on the Heartbreak Ridge Trail. North of this junction, a steady climb leads to the Devils Bathtub Trail, where you'll turn left. This trail works its way west across the slopes at the head of Madrona Canyon, passing seasonal Devils Bathtub Spring. At the Madrona Trail, turn right on the Manning Camp Trail. Less than a mile of climbing leads to Manning Camp, which has a ranger station, another designated campground, and a permanent spring set in a fine stand of old-growth ponderosa pine.

Just north of the ranger station, you have a choice of two trails: Turn left on the Cow Head Saddle Trail, which climbs around the heads of two drainages through mixed pine and oak before reaching another trail junction. Turn right on the Fire Loop Trail and hike northeast through open ponderosa pine and Douglas fir forest past Spud Rock Trail to Mica Mountain, the highest summit in the Rincon Mountains at 8,664 feet. Mica Mountain, the site of a former fire lookout tower, has a rounded, forested summit and little in the way of views.

Stay left on the Fire Loop Trail past the Mica Mountain Trail and then turn right on the Bonita Trail. This trail descends a gently sloping ridge south through open stands of ponderosa and limber pine, then crosses Mica Meadow to meet the Fire Loop Trail once again. Here you can take a 0.2-mile walk east to the spectacular viewpoint at Reef Rock. Back at the south end of the Bonita Trail, head southwest on the Fire Loop Trail, staying left at another trail junction. After the Fire Loop Trail passes Man Head, a huge rounded boulder, it drops down to meet the Heartbreak Ridge Trail. Turn left and follow the Heartbreak Ridge Trail as it descends southeast to yet another junction, where you'll turn left onto the Switchback Trail. This short trail descends off the main ridge and ends at the East Slope Trail, where you'll turn left and hike north to the junction with a 0.1-mile spur trail. The spur trail leads north to Spud Rock

Campground and seasonal Spud Rock Spring, set in a fine ponderosa-pine-and-aspen glade.

From the junction near the campground, follow the trail, now the Deer Head Spring Trail, as it descends south along the east slopes of the mountain to the Turkey Creek Trail. Turn left here and follow the trail past seasonal Deer Head Spring. The Turkey Creek Trail descends steeply through mixed ponderosa pine and chaparral brush. Because the Turkey Creek Trail is not nearly as steep and rocky as the Miller Creek Trail, it's an alternate route for the Arizona Trail and is usable by horses. As you descend, the tall pines disappear, to be replaced by pinyon-juniper woodland. Mudhole Spring is located next to the trail. Watch for cut stone work along the trail. Near the base of the mountain, you'll reencounter high desert grassland and the view opens out. The trail crosses a saddle at the head of Turkey Creek, passes the national park boundary, then works its way southeast along a grassy ridge east of Turkey Creek. The trail becomes a four-wheel-drive road; follow the road southeast along the ridge. After the road turns south and drops into Turkey Creek, it meets the Turkey Creek Trailhead. Follow the main road south to FR 35, and then turn right and walk to the Miller Creek Trailhead turnoff. A short walk up this road leads to the Miller Creek Trailhead, completing the loop.

MILES AND DIRECTIONS

0.0 Start at the Miller Creek Trailhead.

3.4 Turn right at the Heartbreak Ridge Trail.

6.5 Stay left at Deer Head Spring Trail.

7.0 At the junction of the East Slope and Heartbreak Ridge Trails, turn left on Devils Bathtub Trail.

7.6 Arrive at Devils Bathtub Spring.

8.1 At Madrona Trail, turn right on Manning Camp Trail.

8.9 At Manning Camp and Spring, turn left on Cow Head Saddle Trail.

9.5 Turn right on Fire Loop Trail.

10.2 At Spud Rock Trail, stay left on Fire Loop Trail.

10.5 Arrive at Mica Mountain.

10.7 At Mica Mountain Trail, stay left on the Fire Loop Trail.

10.8 Turn right on the Bonita Trail.

11.5 Turn right on Fire Loop Trail.

11.6 Stay left on Fire Loop Trail.

12.0 Turn left on Heartbreak Ridge Trail.

12.8 Turn left on Switchback Trail.

Manning Camp, with its ranger station and reliable spring, is one of six designated backcountry campsites in the Rincon Mountains.

13.1 Turn left on East Slope Trail.

13.2 At Spud Rock Spring and Campground, turn right on Deer Head Spring Trail.

13.6 Turn left on Turkey Creek Trail.

14.8 Arrive at Mudhole Spring.

17.6 The trail becomes a 4WD road.

19.4 At Turkey Creek Trailhead, follow the main road.

19.6 Turn right on FR 35.

20.0 Turn right on the road to Miller Creek Trailhead.

20.2 Arrive at Miller Creek Trailhead.

HIGHLIGHTS: A long day hike or overnight hike to the second-highest summit in the Rincon Mountains. Although the climb to Rincon Peak and return can be done in one long day, it is more enjoyable to do the trip as a two- or even three-day backpack trip, using Happy Valley Campground as a base camp for a day hike up Rincon Peak.

TYPE OF TRIP: Out-and-back.

DISTANCE: 13 miles.

DIFFICULTY: Difficult.

PERMITTED USES: Hiking.

MAPS: Saguaro National Park National Geographic.

SPECIAL CONSIDERATIONS: During the hot summer weather, hikers should carry plenty of water on this long hike, which gains 4,200 feet. Backpacking is most enjoyable during April and May when the spring at Happy Valley Campground usually has water.

PARKING AND FACILITIES: Dirt parking area; no facilities.

FINDING THE TRAILHEAD: From the Rincon Visitor Center, turn left onto Old Spanish Trail, drive 0.2 mile, then turn right (west) on Escalante Road. Continue 2 miles, then turn left on Houghton Road. Drive south 8.1 miles, then turn left onto Interstate 10 via the I–10 East ramp. After 21.4 miles on I–10, exit at Mescal Road/J-Six Ranch and then turn left on Mescal Road. Initially paved, Mescal Road becomes graded dirt and is marked Forest Road 35. Except after a storm, the road is passable to passenger cars if driven with care. About 15.4 miles from I–10, turn left into the signed Miller Creek Trailhead.

From the trailhead, follow the Miller Creek Trail up Miller Creek and west through the Rincon Mountains foothills. After passing the Saguaro National Park boundary, the trail starts to climb the steep eastern slopes of the Rincon Mountains in a series of broad switchbacks. The trail is rocky and steep in places as it works its way through complex terrain with granite cliffs, large boulders, and chaparral brush. Pinyon pines and junipers start to appear as you climb, and the view of the wild country to the east expands. After the trail swings into a nameless canyon and climbs along a north-facing slope, you'll encounter a few ponderosa pines. The canyon bottom sometimes has water, especially in the spring.

When the trail reaches the ridge crest, it meets the Heartbreak Ridge and Rincon Peak Trails south of Happy Valley Saddle. Turn left and hike 0.4 mile

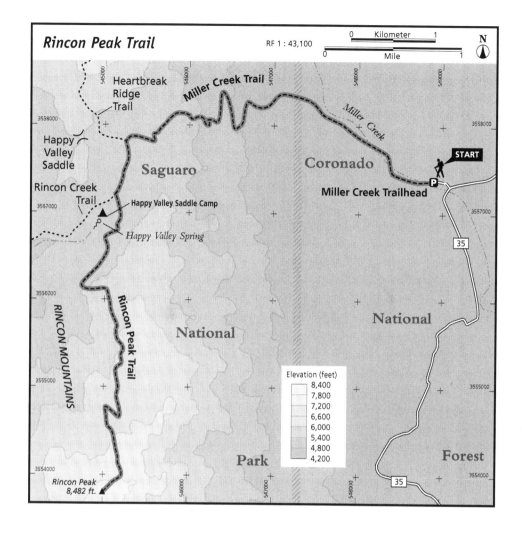

Rincon Peak Trail

RF 1 : 43,100

Kilometer

Mile

N

Heartbreak Ridge Trail

Miller Creek Trail

Miller Creek

START

Happy Valley Saddle

Saguaro

Coronado

Rincon Creek Trail

Happy Valley Saddle Camp

Miller Creek Trailhead

P

35

Happy Valley Spring

RINCON MOUNTAINS

Rincon Peak Trail

National

National

Elevation (feet)

| 8,400 |
| 7,800 |
| 7,200 |
| 6,600 |
| 6,000 |
| 5,400 |
| 4,800 |
| 4,200 |

Park

Forest

35

Rincon Peak 8,482 ft.

south to the Rincon Creek Trail and Happy Valley Campground, with its seasonal spring. The campground is set in a fine stand of old-growth ponderosa pine.

Stay left on the Rincon Peak Trail and hike south as the trail works its way up generally west-facing slopes. As the trail begins to climb more steeply through the mixed chaparral and pinyon-juniper woodland, the views, especially to the west, become better. The gradual ascent continues as you reach the first Douglas fir trees. At about 7,400 feet the trail starts the final, steep ascent of the north ridge of Rincon Peak, and stock are not allowed beyond this point. The steep rocky trail finally arrives on the bald, exposed summit of Rincon Peak itself, marked by a huge rock cairn.

Rincon Peak from Happy Valley Lookout

As you would expect, and certainly deserve after the climb, the views from this 8,482-foot summit are stunning, taking in many of the isolated mountain ranges of southeast Arizona. One of the more remote ranges is visible to the northeast, the Galiuro Mountains, and slightly to the east, the long 10,000-foot ridge of the Pinaleno Mountains, topped by the distinctive white box of the Mount Graham Observatory. Directly east lies the white Willcox Playa, and more to the southeast you can spot the rugged granite ridges of the Dragoon Mountains and Cochise Stronghold, one of the hideouts of the legendary Chiricahua Apache chief. Beyond the Dragoons the 9,000-foot ridge of the Chiricahua Mountains rises near the New Mexico border. To the south-southeast another 9,000-foot range, the Huachucas, is visible and beyond, the mountains and deserts of northern Sonora, Mexico.

MILES AND DIRECTIONS

0.0 Begin at the Miller Creek Trailhead.

3.2 At the Heartbreak Ridge Trail, turn left on the Rincon Peak Trail.

3.6 At the Rincon Creek Trail and Happy Valley Saddle Campground, stay left on the Rincon Peak Trail.

6.5 Arrive at Rincon Peak.

13.0 Return to the Miller Creek Trailhead.

Santa Catalina Mountains

Rising to the north and east of Tucson, the Santa Catalina Mountains are the largest, highest, and most complex of the three mountain ranges next to Tucson. Elevations range from 2,700 feet at the base of the mountains to 9,157-foot Mount Lemmon, so like the Rincon Mountains, the Catalinas encompass four distinct life zones from Lower Sonoran cacti and scrub to the Canadian mixed conifer and aspen on the summits and northeast slopes.

The steep ridges and rugged peaks rising from the desert floor and forming the northern skyline of Tucson are not actually the highest portion of the Santa Catalina Mountains but almost a separate range divided from the higher Mount Lemmon area by Sabino and Romero Canyons. Known locally as the Front Range, these deep canyons and rocky peaks are part of the Pusch Ridge Wilderness and are accessible only by trail.

Catalina State Park lies along the Canada del Oro at the west side of the range and provides access to several Catalina trailheads. In addition, the park has a trail system of its own, as well as picnic areas and a campground.

A ridge running southeast from Mount Lemmon forms the high crest of the Santa Catalinas, including several summits above 8,000 feet. In contrast to the rocky peaks of the Front Range, the crest area is relatively gentle. The Catalina Highway takes advantage of this terrain to more or less follow the crest to Mount Lemmon and provides easy access to the upper part of the mountain.

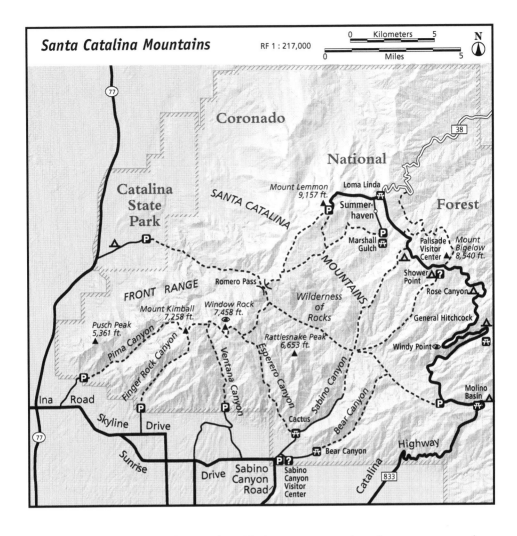

RF 1 : 217,000

0   Kilometers   5

0   Miles   5

N

Coronado

National

Forest

Catalina
State
Park

SANTA CATALINA

Mount Lemmon
9,157 ft.

Loma Linda

Summer-
haven

Marshall
Gulch

Palisade
Visitor
Center

Mount
Bigelow
8,540 ft.

Shower
Point

Rose Canyon

FRONT RANGE

Romero Pass

Wilderness
of
Rocks

MOUNTAINS

General Hitchcock

Mount Kimball
7,258 ft.

Window Rock
7,458 ft.

Pusch Peak
5,361 ft.

Rattlesnake Peak
6,653 ft.

Pima Canyon

Finger Rock Canyon

Ventana Canyon

Esperero Canyon

Sabino Canyon

Bear Canyon

Windy Point

Molino
Basin

Ina   Road

Skyline   Drive

Cactus

Sunrise

Drive

Sabino
Canyon
Road

Sabino
Canyon
Visitor
Center

Bear Canyon

Catalina

Highway

833

West and south of the Catalina Highway, canyons drop into more rugged country, such as the Wilderness of Rocks, much of which is in the northern and eastern portion of the Pusch Ridge Wilderness.

The remaining sections of the Catalinas are the more remote north and east slopes, lying below the Catalina Highway. The original summit road, the Old Mount Lemmon Road, climbs these slopes to the top.

The Santa Catalinas are a hiker's and backpacker's paradise, and cross-country skiers and snowshoers often have enough snow around Mount Lemmon during the winter to pursue their activities. Rock climbing is very popular on a number of granitic crags near the Catalina Highway. See appendix B for guide books. The Summit Hut in Tucson at 5041 East Speedway (800–499–8696; www.summithut.com) is the best source of current climbing information.

Getting to the Santa Catalinas

To reach Catalina State Park from Interstate 10 north, take the Tangerine Road exit and head east 13.6 miles. Turn right on Arizona Highway 77, the Oracle Highway, and drive 0.9 mile south to the park entrance, which is on the left.

Several trailheads are located along the foot of the Front Range between Catalina State Park and Sabino Canyon Visitor Center. These are reached by city streets and are described in the "Trails" section later in the chapter.

To reach the Sabino Canyon Visitor Center from I–10 north, exit at Ina Road and head east. After 5.6 miles turn right on Skyline Drive. In 3.2 miles stay right as the main road becomes Sunrise Drive. Continue east 6.4 miles to Sabino Canyon Road and turn left, then immediately right into the Sabino Canyon parking lot. There is a fee for parking here.

To reach the Sabino Canyon Visitor Center from Tucson, head north on Sabino Canyon Road. Just after Sunrise Drive, turn right into the Sabino Canyon parking lot.

Mount Lemmon and the summit area are reached via the Catalina Highway. From I–10, exit at Speedway Boulevard and drive east 7.3 miles. Turn left on Wilmot Road, go north 0.4 mile, and then turn right on Tanque Verde Road. Continue 3.8 miles and then turn left on Catalina Highway. It is approximately 31 miles to Mount Lemmon. After the road enters the Coronado National Forest, there is an entrance station where you can pay the required fee.

The main access route in the Santa Catalinas is the Catalina Highway, which leads from northeast Tucson to the top of the range. As described in the next section, trailheads along the foothills are accessible from Tucson. Since there is no public transport, you will need a car to explore the Santa Catalina Mountains.

Finding the Trailheads

There are several trailheads on the west and south sides of the Santa Catalina Mountains, generally at the mouths of major canyons draining the Front Range. All these trailheads, except for those at Catalina State Park and Sabino Canyon Recreation Area, are on private land and parking is extremely limited, especially on weekends. Other trailheads are reached from the Catalina Highway at various places along the road's ascent to Mount Lemmon. These trailheads are on national forest land.

Since the Sabino Canyon Visitor Center is a good place to start your exploration of the Catalinas, I use it as a starting point for instructions on finding other trailheads. If you're not starting from the Sabino Canyon Visitor Center, use a map of Tucson to intercept the route at a major intersection.

Visitor Centers and Amenities

The Sabino Canyon Visitor Center, in the Sabino Canyon Recreation Area at the north end of Sabino Canyon Road, is a good starting point for learning about the Santa Catalina Mountains. The visitor center has exhibits, a bookstore, and a nearby nature trail. Two shuttles (fee required) operate daily and run to the end of the Sabino and Bear Canyon Roads, providing access to picnic areas, scenic overlooks, and trailheads.

Palisade Visitor Center is located at milepost 19.1 on the Catalina Highway. Exhibits explain the natural and human history of the Santa Catalina Mountains, and a bookstore has books and videos. One of the exhibits is a slice from an old Douglas fir that dates back to 1672. Various events in Arizona history are noted on the tree rings.

Since the Catalina Mountains lie at the northeast side of Tucson, access to the city is easy, and all amenities are available, including motels, hotels, bed-and-breakfast inns, and resorts.

Campgrounds

Catalina State Park, at the western foot of the range, has a campground with forty-eight units, half with electric and water hookups. Peppersauce is a seventeen-site Forest Service campground located in the the northern foothills, south of Oracle. There are five Forest Service campgrounds located along the Catalina Highway, including Molino Basin, Prison Camp, General Hitchcock, Rose Canyon, and Spencer Canyon Campgrounds. These range in size from eight to seventy-four sites. Backcountry camping is allowed in the Pusch Ridge Wilderness and most of the Coronado National Forest.

Scenic Drives

Catalina Highway

HIGHLIGHTS: There are opportunities for picnicking, camping, and stopping at scenic overlooks on this drive.

TYPE OF TRIP: One-way.

DISTANCE: 31 miles.

The Catalina Highway starts in Tucson, from East Tanque Verde Road just east of Pantano Road, and climbs about 31 miles to Mount Lemmon. There is a fee for use of this paved road, payable at the entrance station. There are several campgrounds (see above) and picnic areas, as well as scenic overlooks, along the drive. The drive is pleasant any time of year, though in winter you may encounter ice and snow on the upper portion of the road, as well as snowstorms and other winter weather. The following is a general description of the Catalina Highway—for specific trailhead directions, see the "Trails" section.

The initial portion of the Catalina Highway heads northwest across what is now a built-up part of the Tucson area but soon reaches the base of the Santa Catalina Mountains and climbs into the mouth of Soldier Canyon. The road then winds along south-facing slopes before heading into Molino Canyon, where you'll pass through the entrance station. (There is a self-payment station if the entrance station is closed.) Next, the road passes through Molino Basin, where there is a picnic area and campground. As the road turns west, you'll be passing through the Upper Sonoran life zone, where the saguaros have disappeared and desert grassland has taken over. You'll pass the old prison camp site, on the right, where the prisoners who built the Catalina Highway stayed. Prison Camp is a trailhead and is being developed into a recreation site.

Next, the road climbs north and east into Bear Canyon, where it passes the Bear Canyon Picnic Area and General Hitchcock Campground near the head of the canyon. Now the road bends back on itself, climbing southwest along the canyon wall, then swinging around Windy Point Vista and Geology Vista, two of the most spectacular viewpoints along the Catalina Highway. The road finally arrives at the crest of the Santa Catalinas near Green Mountain, passing the Rose Canyon Campground turnoff on the left, followed by the San Pedro Vista. Here you can get a look at the "other side" of the Catalinas—the northeast slopes dropping steeply into the San Pedro Valley. The Catalina Highway now heads generally northwest just below the crest, passing the Palisade Visitor Center (open seasonally) below Mount Bigelow. Mount Bigelow is home to numerous radio and television broadcast towers, as well as a Forest Service fire lookout. Next, you'll pass the Spencer Canyon Campground and Bear Wallow Picnic Area, after which the road runs along the crest. You'll pass the Syke Knob, Inspiration Rock, and Loma Linda Picnic Areas, followed by the Old Mount Lemmon Road (Forest Road 38) on the right. Next on the left comes the turnoff to Summerhaven (the mountaintop summer-home community) and the Marshall Gulch Picnic Area and Trailhead.

The Catalina Highway continues west past Mount Lemmon Ski Valley and several trailheads to end atop Mount Lemmon, the summit of the range. The actual summit is home to an observatory and is closed to public access.

Sabino and Bear Canyon Shuttles

Although you can't drive your own vehicle on the Sabino and Bear Canyon Roads, the shuttles are a better way to see both canyons. You can get tickets for either shuttle at the Sabino Canyon Visitor Center. Both shuttle routes have numerous stops where you can get off the shuttle, take a walk, or have a picnic at any of several sites. Some people walk the road between the shuttle stops, then board the shuttle to continue. As with other activities in the desert foothills, early morning is the best time to enjoy these canyons during the summer months.

Trails

Romero Canyon Trail

HIGHLIGHTS: A long day hike or backpack trip into the Pusch Ridge Wilderness from Catalina State Park, ending at Romero Pass at the head of Romero Canyon.

TYPE OF TRIP: Out-and-back.

DISTANCE: 12 miles.

DIFFICULTY: Difficult.

PERMITTED USES: Hiking, horseback riding.

MAPS: Pusch Ridge Wilderness USFS.

SPECIAL CONSIDERATIONS: This hike has 3,230 feet of elevation gain. Carry plenty of water during the hot summer months.

PARKING AND FACILITIES: Paved parking area at Catalina State Park, which has restrooms, picnic areas, and camping.

FINDING THE TRAILHEAD: From Sabino Canyon Visitor Center, turn left on Sabino Canyon Road, then immediately right on Sunrise Drive. After 6.4 miles Sunrise becomes Skyline Drive; continue west another 1.9 miles and then turn left on Ina Road. After 1.7 miles turn right on Oracle Road (Arizona Highway 77). Continue north 6.2 miles and then turn right into Catalina State Park (there is a fee for entry). Drive 1.8 miles on the main park road to the Romero Canyon Trailhead, on the left.

From the trailhead, cross the road and follow the broad trail across normally dry Sutherland Wash. The hiking is easy, with great views of the Front Range, until you reach the base of the mountains, where the Romero Canyon Trail starts to climb in earnest. After climbing for a shorter distance than you expect, the trail turns southeast and contours through a saddle before descending into Romero Canyon. Seasonal pools of water along this section of Romero Canyon are known as Romero Pools. Spring is the best time to find water at this popular spot.

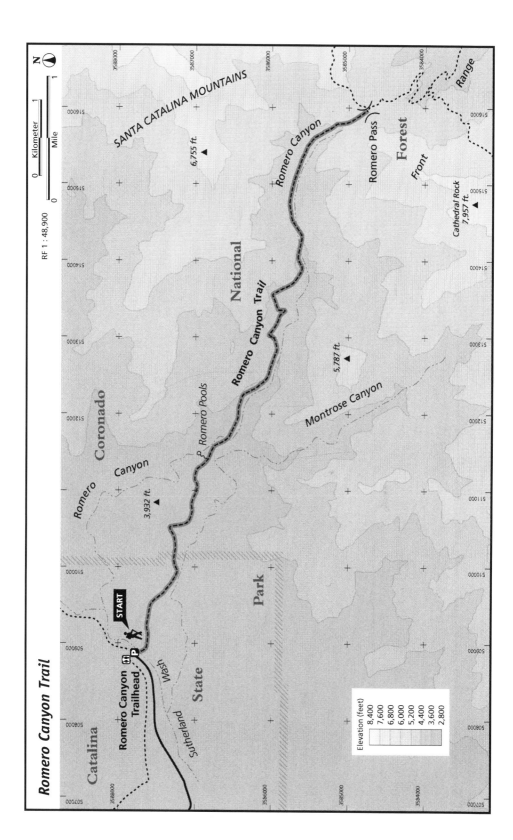

Beyond the pools, the trail is less traveled as it stays north of the bed of Romero Canyon, climbing to the southeast. A steep ascent with several switchbacks marks the beginning of a mile-long section where the trail climbs well above the canyon bottom. The Romero Canyon Trail returns to the bed of Romero Canyon and follows the upper section of the canyon east and then southeast for the final ascent to Romero Pass, the goal for this hike. The pass

Santa Catalina Front Range from Romero Canyon Trail

is on the crest of the Front Range and offers views of the Santa Catalina high country to the northeast.

Backpackers wishing to continue into the wilder sections of the Pusch Ridge Wilderness can connect to trails leading to the top of Mount Lemmon, down the West Fork of Sabino Canyon, and into Front Range canyons including Esperero, Ventana, Finger Rock, and Pima Canyons.

MILES AND DIRECTIONS

0.0 Begin at the Romero Canyon Trailhead.

1.1 Begin the climb at the foothills.

2.3 Descend into Romero Canyon.

6.0 Make the final ascent to Romero Pass.

12.0 Return to the Romero Canyon Trailhead.

Pima Canyon Trail

HIGHLIGHTS: A scenic route into the Pusch Ridge Wilderness to the summit of Mount Kimball, a prominent peak in the Front Range of the Santa Catalina Mountains.

TYPE OF TRIP: Out-and-back.

DISTANCE: 10.8 miles.

DIFFICULTY: Difficult.

PERMITTED USES: Hiking, horseback riding.

MAPS: Pusch Ridge Wilderness USFS.

SPECIAL CONSIDERATIONS: This hike has 4,240 feet of elevation gain. Carry plenty of water during the hot summer months.

PARKING AND FACILITIES: Small paved parking area; no facilities.

FINDING THE TRAILHEAD: From Sabino Canyon Visitor Center, turn left on Sabino Canyon Road, then immediately right on Sunrise Drive. After 6.4 miles Sunrise becomes Skyline Drive; continue west another 1.9 miles and then turn left on Ina Road. After 0.7 mile, turn right on Christie Drive. Continue north and northeast 1.4 miles, then turn right and drive 0.2 mile to the Pima Canyon Trailhead.

The first section of the Pima Canyon Trail is on private land and is closely bordered by fences; please stay on the trail. After the trail enters the national forest and the Pusch Ridge Wilderness, it more or less follows the bottom of Pima

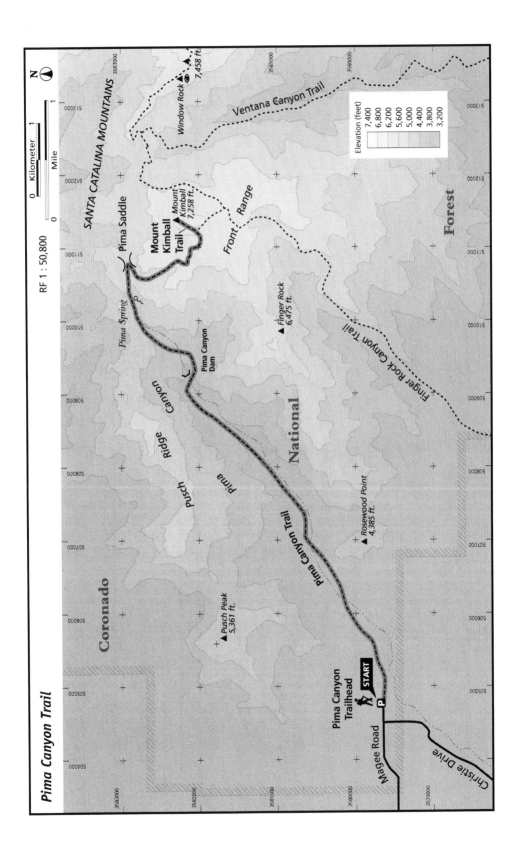

Pima Canyon Trail

RF 1 : 50,800

N

SANTA CATALINA MOUNTAINS

Window Rock
7,458 ft.

Ventana Canyon Trail

Pima Saddle

Mount Kimball
7,258 ft.

Mount Kimball Trail

Front Range

Pima Spring

Finger Rock
6,475 ft.

Pima Canyon Dam

Pusch Ridge Canyon

Finger Rock Canyon Trail

Pima

Pima Canyon Trail

National

Rosewood Point
4,385 ft.

Coronado

Pusch Peak
5,361 ft.

Forest

Pima Canyon Trailhead

START

P

Magee Road

Christie Drive

Elevation (feet)
7,400
6,800
6,200
5,600
5,000
4,400
3,800
3,200

0   Kilometer   1

0   Mile   1

Canyon as the canyon climbs northeast into the Front Range. Lower Pima Canyon is in the Lower Sonoran life zone, marked by saguaro, prickly pear, cholla, and barrel cacti, mesquite bushes, catclaw, and paloverde trees.

During the spring after snowmelt, the creek is often running, and later in the year there will still be seasonal pools, which are popular destinations during the hot summer months.

At first you'll have views of Tucson and the Santa Rita Mountains to the south, but as you continue the ascent of Pima Canyon past Rosewood Point, the view becomes blocked by the twists and turns of the canyon. In less than 2 miles of hiking, you've left the city behind, out of sight and earshot, and have entered remote wilderness.

After about 2 miles the trail becomes fainter and more brushy. The crags above Pima Canyon are prime bighorn-sheep country, and you may see one up high on seemingly inaccessible ledges. I've found the best way to find them is to search carefully with binoculars during rest stops. You may sometimes hear them moving if the wind is calm and you are silent.

About 3 miles up the canyon, you'll come to Pima Canyon Dam, a small masonry structure built by the Arizona Game and Fish Department as a source of water for wildlife. In the upper canyon you'll gradually enter the Upper Sonoran life zone, characterized by grassland and oaks.

Seasonal Pima Spring marks the start of the final, steep ascent to a trail junction just below Pima Saddle at the head of Pima Canyon. A spur trail leads to the saddle; stay on the main trail as it turns sharply southwest, then heads southeast up a tributary canyon, finally climbing a ridge onto Mount Kimball. This is a rough and rocky trail that climbs very steeply—allow plenty of time for this section. Up here you are in the Transition life zone, marked by tall ponderosa pines.

Turn left on a short spur trail to reach the summit of Mount Kimball, which offers sweeping views of the Front Range around you, Tucson and the desert plains to the south and west, and the Mount Lemmon and Santa Catalina high country to the northeast.

MILES AND DIRECTIONS

0.0 Begin at the Pima Canyon Trailhead.

3.0 Arrive at the Pima Canyon Dam.

4.2 Pima Spring marks the start of a steep ascent.

4.5 This is where Pima Saddle is located.

5.3 Turn left on the Mount Kimball Trail.

5.4 Arrive at the summit of Mount Kimball.

10.8 Return to the trailhead.

HIGHLIGHTS: An alternative route to the summit of Mount Kimball, using the trail up Finger Rock Canyon. This trail is shorter than the Pima Canyon Trail.

TYPE OF TRIP: Out-and-back.

DISTANCE: 8 miles.

DIFFICULTY: Difficult.

PERMITTED USES: Hiking, horseback riding.

MAPS: Pusch Ridge Wilderness USFS.

SPECIAL CONSIDERATIONS: This hike has 4,110 feet of elevation gain. Carry plenty of water during the hot summer months as the trail stays well above the canyon bottom with little access to seasonal water.

PARKING AND FACILITIES: Small paved parking area; no facilities.

Finger Rock, Santa Catalina Mountains

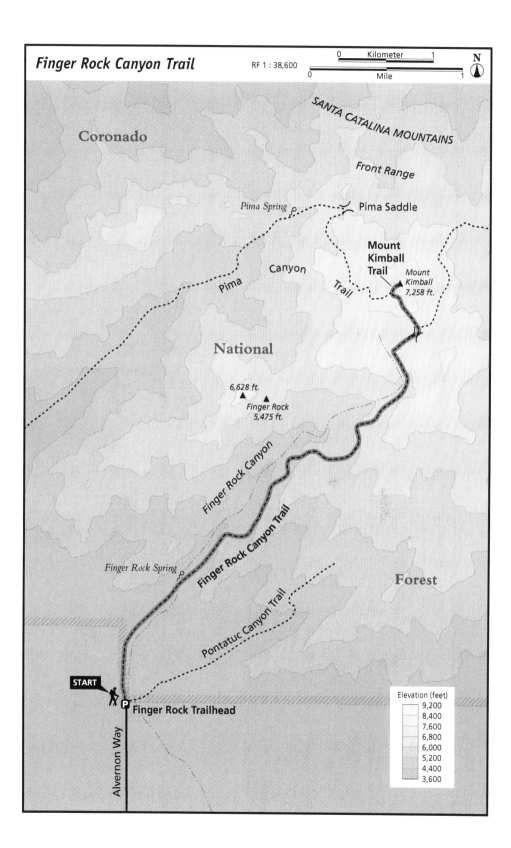

FINDING THE TRAILHEAD: From Sabino Canyon Visitor Center, turn left on Sabino Canyon Road, then immediately right on Sunrise Drive. After 4.3 miles turn right on Swan Drive. Drive north 1 mile, turn left on Skyline Drive, drive 1 mile west, and then turn right on Alvernon Way. Continue north 0.9 mile to the Finger Rock Trailhead.

From the Finger Rock Trailhead, walk a few feet north up the road to the Finger Rock Trail, which heads north along the national forest boundary into the mouth of spectacular Finger Rock Canyon. The trail climbs the gentle slopes at the mouth of the canyon through typical Lower Sonoran vegetation—catclaw, mesquite, and saguaro and cholla cacti. Once in Finger Rock Canyon, the trail turns northeast and generally follows the bed of the canyon, passing seasonal Finger Rock Spring and seasonal pools along the way. After Finger Rock Spring, the trail climbs along the east slopes of Finger Rock Canyon, not dropping into the bed of the canyon again until near the head of the canyon. Finger Rock is clearly visible on the skyline to the north.

A final steep climb leads to a saddle, where you'll turn left on the Pima Canyon Trail. A short ascent to the northwest leads to the rounded top of Mount Kimball. Turn right on a short spur trail to reach the actual summit with its 360-degree views of the Front Range, the main Santa Catalina Mountains to the northeast, and, of course, Tucson and the desert valleys to the south and west.

MILES AND DIRECTIONS

0.0 Begin at the Finger Rock Trailhead.

1.0 Pass Finger Rock Spring.

3.6 Turn left on the Pima Canyon Trail.

3.9 Turn right on the Mount Kimball Trail.

4.0 Arrive at the Mount Kimball summit.

8.0 Return to the Finger Rock Trailhead.

Ventana Canyon Trail

HIGHLIGHTS: A hike up a rugged canyon to Window Rock, in the front range of the Santa Catalina Mountains.

TYPE OF TRIP: Out-and-back.

DISTANCE: 10.8 miles.

DIFFICULTY: Difficult.

PERMITTED USES: Hiking, horseback riding.

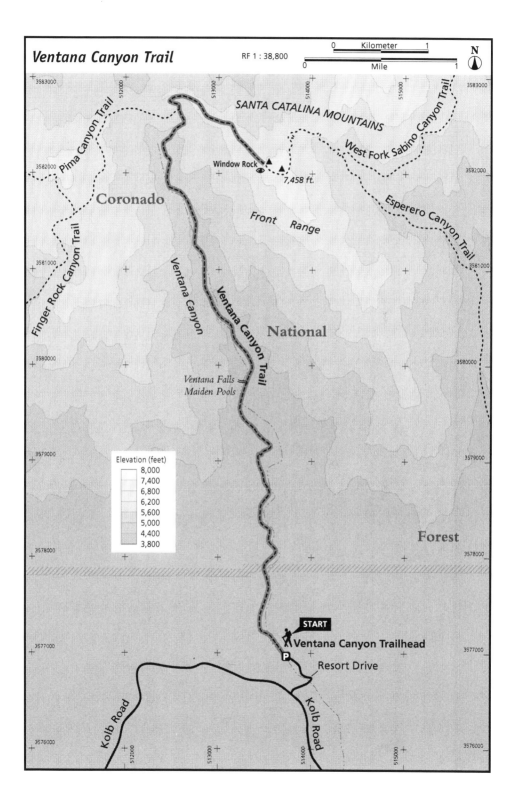

MAPS: Pusch Ridge Wilderness USFS.

SPECIAL CONSIDERATIONS: This hike has 4,040 feet of elevation gain. Carry plenty of water during the hot summer months.

PARKING AND FACILITIES: Small paved parking area; no facilities.

FINDING THE TRAILHEAD: From Sabino Canyon Visitor Center, turn left on Sabino Canyon Road, then immediately right on Sunrise Drive. After 1.3 miles turn right on Kolb Road. Continue north 1.4 miles, then turn right on Resort Drive. Park in the signed trailhead parking lot.

The Ventana Canyon Trail heads northwest from the parking area and is closely fenced on both sides as it crosses private land. Be sure to stay on the trail through this section. After entering the mouth of Ventana Canyon, the trail crosses the forest and wilderness boundary. Staying close to the bed of the canyon except in one place about 0.7 mile from the forest boundary, the trail follows Ventana Canyon generally north into the Front Range. In the lower portion of the canyon, saguaro cacti, mesquite, and cholla cacti show that you are in the Lower Sonoran life zone. Ventana Canyon is narrow with steep walls towering on either side, topped with craggy rock outcrops and cliffs. Seasonal pools grace the canyon floor; they usually run after spring snowmelt.

About 2 miles up the canyon, you'll reach Ventana Falls and Maiden Pools. When they are running, Ventana Falls are some of the best in the range. Above Maiden Pools the trail becomes more overgrown with brush and less distinct.

At the head of the canyon, the trail climbs steeply to the northeast, meeting the Pima Canyon Trail. Stay right and follow the Ventana Canyon Trail southeast along the ridge to Window Rock, the canyon's namesake formation (*ventana* means "window" in Spanish). The final climb is steep and rocky, but the view is worth it.

MILES AND DIRECTIONS

0.0 Start at the Ventana Canyon Trailhead.

2.0 Reach Ventana Falls and Maiden Pools.

4.4 At Pima Canyon Trail, stay right on Ventana Canyon Trail.

5.4 Arrive at Window Rock.

10.8 Return to the trailhead.

HIGHLIGHTS: This rugged trail takes you into one of the more remote Front Range canyons to a seasonal waterfall.

TYPE OF TRIP: Out-and-back.

DISTANCE: 10.6 miles.

DIFFICULTY: Difficult.

PERMITTED USES: Hiking, horseback riding.

MAPS: Pusch Ridge Wilderness USFS.

SPECIAL CONSIDERATIONS: Although there is seasonal water in Esperero Canyon, carry plenty of water, especially during the hot summer months.

PARKING AND FACILITIES: Large parking area (fee) at Sabino Canyon Visitor Center with restrooms and the Sabino and Bear Canyon Shuttles.

FINDING THE TRAILHEAD: Start at the Sabino Canyon Visitor Center.

From the visitor center, walk up the Sabino Canyon Road to the Cactus Picnic Area and turn left onto the Esperero Canyon Trail. The trail starts climbing almost immediately, skirting the lower portion of Rattlesnake Canyon. A short climb leads over a ridge and into Bird Canyon, where the trail skirts the forest and wilderness boundary. As usual, housing developments have been built right up to the forest boundary. The Esperero Canyon Trail starts to climb seriously, crossing the ridge west of Bird Canyon. It then climbs up an unnamed tributary of Bird Canyon to reach a saddle, known as "Cardiac Gap," overlooking Esperero Canyon. By this point, you've left the saguaro cacti and mesquite brush of the Lower Sonoran life zone behind and have entered the oak grasslands of the Upper Sonoran.

For a short distance, the trail descends along the east canyon wall, but then resumes the inevitable climb, not actually reaching the floor of its namesake canyon until Geronimo Meadow, apparently named because it is about the only somewhat-level place in an otherwise narrow, steep canyon. As you continue north up Esperero Canyon, the trail stays pretty much in the bed. About a mile north of Geronimo Meadow, the trail comes to Bridal Veil Falls, a seasonal 40-foot waterfall, which is the goal for this hike.

The trail continues to Window Rock and connects with the Ventana Canyon and Pima Canyon Trails, but the upper section of the trail is little used.

MILES AND DIRECTIONS

0.0 Start at the Sabino Canyon Visitor Center.

1.2 At the Cactus Picnic Area, turn left onto the Esperero Canyon Trail.

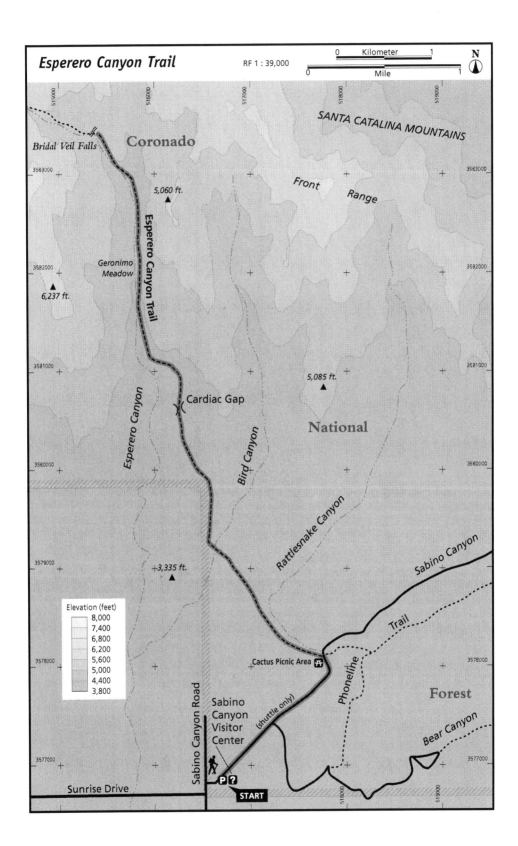

Esperero Canyon Trail

RF 1 : 39,000

Kilometer 0 — 1

Mile 0 — 1

N

SANTA CATALINA MOUNTAINS

Bridal Veil Falls

Coronado

5,060 ft.

Front Range

Esperero Canyon Trail

Geronimo Meadow

6,237 ft.

5,085 ft.

Esperero Canyon

Cardiac Gap

National

Bird Canyon

Rattlesnake Canyon

Sabino Canyon

+3,335 ft.

Trail

Elevation (feet)
8,000
7,400
6,800
6,200
5,600
5,000
4,400
3,800

Cactus Picnic Area

Phoneline

Forest

Sabino Canyon Road

Sabino Canyon Visitor Center

(shuttle only)

Bear Canyon

Sunrise Drive

START

4.1 You're overlooking Esperero Canyon.

4.3 Arrive at Geronimo Meadow.

5.3 Arrive at Bridal Veil Falls.

10.6 Retrace your steps back to the visitor center.

Sabino Canyon Trail

HIGHLIGHTS: A hike up dramatic Sabino Canyon and its west fork to Hutch's Pool, a series of pools that are swimmable when they exist in spring and early summer.

TYPE OF TRIP: Out-and-back.

DISTANCE: 6.8 miles.

DIFFICULTY: Moderate.

PERMITTED USES: Hiking.

MAPS: Pusch Ridge Wilderness USFS.

SPECIAL CONSIDERATIONS: During the hot summer months, plan your hike for early in the morning and carry plenty of water.

PARKING AND FACILITIES: Large parking area (fee) at Sabino Canyon Visitor Center with restrooms and the Sabino and Bear Canyon Shuttles. The trailhead at the end of Sabino Canyon Road is reachable only by shuttle and has restrooms.

FINDING THE TRAILHEAD: From Sabino Canyon Visitor Center, take the Sabino Canyon Shuttle 3.6 miles to the last stop in Sabino Canyon.

From the last shuttle stop in Sabino Canyon, hike north on the Sabino Canyon Trail, which climbs 0.1 mile to meet the Phoneline Trail. Stay left and follow the Sabino Canyon Trail north along the east side of Sabino Canyon to Sabino Basin. Sabino Basin, the confluence of the east and west forks of Sabino Canyon, is a popular camp spot and the start of several trails that head into the Santa Catalina high country to the north.

In Sabino Basin turn left on the West Fork Sabino Canyon Trail. After just 0.1 mile, the Box Camp Trail goes right; stay left. Follow the West Fork Sabino Canyon Trail 1.5 miles west until it veers left away from the bed of the canyon. Turn right on an unmarked, informal trail and hike 0.1 mile up the West Fork to Hutch's Pool.

MILES AND DIRECTIONS

0.0 Begin at the Sabino Canyon Trailhead.

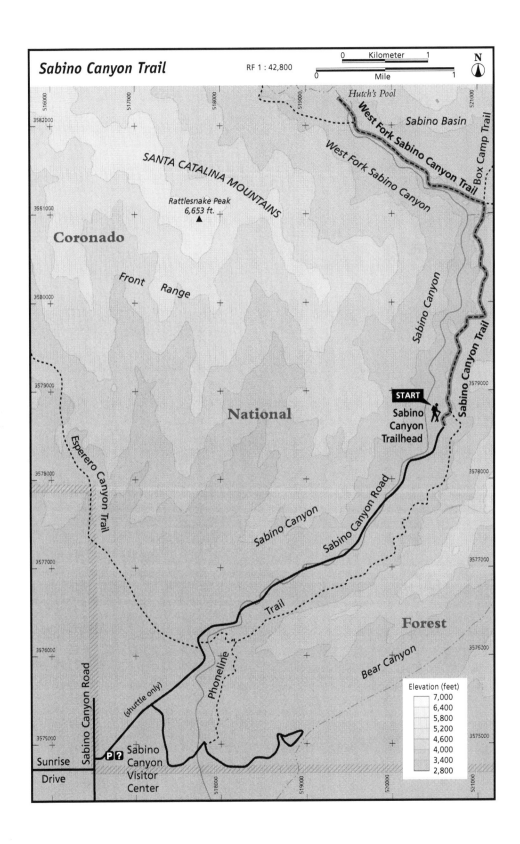

Sabino Canyon Trail

RF 1 : 42,800

Hutch's Pool

Sabino Basin

West Fork Sabino Canyon Trail

West Fork Sabino Canyon

Box Camp Trail

SANTA CATALINA MOUNTAINS

Rattlesnake Peak
6,653 ft.
▲

Coronado

Front Range

Sabino Canyon

Sabino Canyon Trail

National

START

Sabino
Canyon
Trailhead

Esperero Canyon Trail

Sabino Canyon Road

Sabino Canyon

Sabino Canyon Road

Trail

Forest

Bear Canyon

Phoneline

(shuttle only)

Sabino Canyon Road

Sunrise

Drive

🅿❓ Sabino
Canyon
Visitor
Center

Elevation (feet)
	7,000
	6,400
	5,800
	5,200
	4,600
	4,000
	3,400
	2,800

Sabino Canyon in flood, Santa Catalina Mountains

1.7 Turn left on the West Fork Sabino Canyon Trail.

1.8 Stay left on the West Fork Sabino Canyon Trail.

3.3 Turn right on the unmarked trail.

3.4 Arrive at Hutch's Pool.

6.8 Return to the trailhead.

Bear Canyon Trail

HIGHLIGHTS: A walk to famous Seven Falls, a series of seasonal cascades in Bear Canyon.

TYPE OF TRIP: Out-and-back.

DISTANCE: 7 miles.

DIFFICULTY: Moderate.

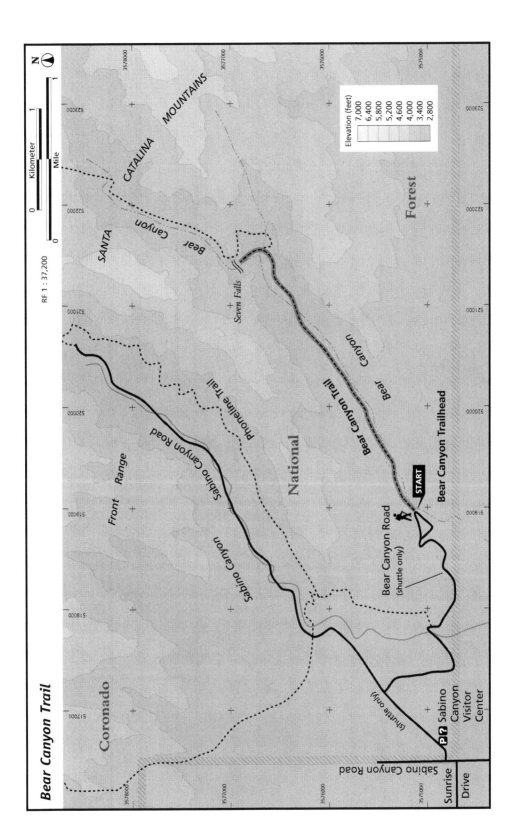

PERMITTED USES: Hiking.

MAPS: Pusch Ridge Wilderness USFS.

SPECIAL CONSIDERATIONS: During the hot summer months, plan your hike for early in the morning and carry plenty of water.

PARKING AND FACILITIES: Large parking area (fee) at Sabino Canyon Visitor Center with restrooms and the Sabino and Bear Canyon Shuttles. The trailhead at the end of Bear Canyon Road is reachable only by shuttle and has a picnic area and restrooms.

FINDING THE TRAILHEAD: From Sabino Canyon Visitor Center, take the Bear Canyon Shuttle 2.5 miles to the Bear Canyon Trailhead at the end of the road.

The extremely popular Bear Canyon Trail heads northeast up rugged Bear Canyon, crossing the seasonal creek numerous times. These crossings may be impossible during heavy spring runoff or after heavy late-summer thunderstorms. About 3 miles up the canyon, the trail switchbacks up the eastern wall, then gradually returns to the streambed. Where the canyon abruptly turns northwest, the trail climbs well above the canyon floor to avoid a series of cascades known locally as the Seven Falls. To explore the falls, leave the trail at the start of this climb and follow the streambed upstream. The falls are at their best after the spring snowmelt, which is usually in late March or into April. Late-summer thunderstorms can also send large amounts of water through the canyon.

The falls are a popular spot and are heavily used. Be extra careful with litter, making certain that you pack everything out.

MILES AND DIRECTIONS

0.0 Begin at the Bear Canyon Trailhead.

3.0 The trail switchbacks up the eastern wall, then returns to the streambed.

3.5 Arrive at Seven Falls.

7.0 Return to the trailhead.

Butterfly Trail

HIGHLIGHTS: A day hike across the northeast slopes of the Santa Catalina Mountains.

TYPE OF TRIP: One-way.

DISTANCE: 6.6 miles.

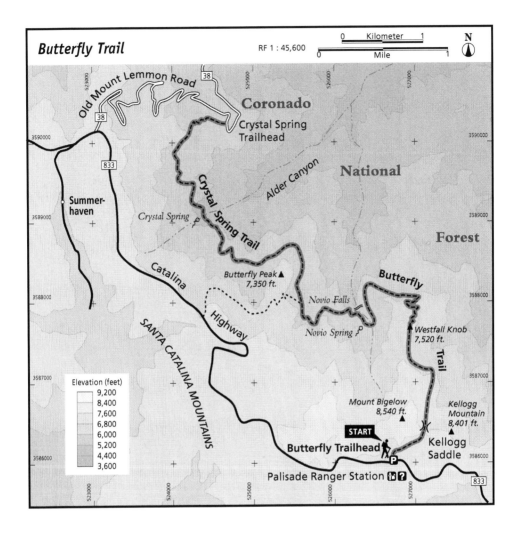

DIFFICULTY: Moderate.

PERMITTED USES: Hiking, horseback riding.

MAPS: Pusch Ridge Wilderness USFS.

SPECIAL CONSIDERATIONS: Although this is a relatively cool and shady hike, carry plenty of water during the warm summer months.

PARKING AND FACILITIES: The Palisade Ranger Station is across the highway.

FINDING THE TRAILHEAD: From the Sabino Canyon Visitor Center, turn left on Sabino Canyon Road, drive south 4.4 miles, and then turn left on Tanque Verde Road. Drive east 2.6 miles and then turn left on Catalina Highway. Stay on the Catalina Highway (a fee is required, payable at the entrance station a few miles into the mountains) 33 miles to the Butterfly Trailhead, on the right. To reach the north trailhead, continue 4.6 miles on the Catalina Highway and then turn right on the Old Mount Lemmon Road. Drive 3 miles on this dirt road to the Crystal Spring Trailhead, which is on the right.

The Butterfly Trail first heads northeast and climbs over Kellogg Saddle, located between Mount Bigelow and Kellogg Mountain, then swings north and descends along an east-facing slope. After passing over Westfall Knob, the trail descends along the ridge in a series of switchbacks, then turns west and contours into a canyon. When the Butterfly Trail crosses the main drainage, watch for Novio Spring, above the trail. There is also a seasonal waterfall in the drainage below the trail. This spot makes a good destination for an out-and-back hike of 5.4 miles.

Beyond Novio Spring the Butterfly Trail continues to descend until it meets the Crystal Spring Trail southeast of Butterfly Peak. At this junction the Butterfly Trail goes left; turn right on the Crystal Spring Trail, which swings around the north slopes of Butterfly Peak and then crosses into the Alder Creek drainage. Crystal Spring is located in the main fork of Alder Creek. After Crystal Spring the trail climbs north along the east-facing slopes of Alder Canyon before descending steeply to end at the Old Mountain Lemmon Road and the north trailhead.

MILES AND DIRECTIONS

0.0 Begin at the South Butterfly Trailhead.

0.4 Climb over the Kellogg Saddle.

1.5 Pass over Westfall Knob.

2.7 Watch for Novio Spring and waterfall.

3.6 Turn right on Crystal Spring Trail.

5.4 Arrive at Crystal Spring.

6.6 The trail ends at the Crystal Spring Trailhead at Old Mount Lemmon Road.

Aspen Trail

HIGHLIGHTS: A short day hike to a viewpoint overlooking the rugged Wilderness of Rocks area.

TYPE OF TRIP: Loop.

DISTANCE: 3 miles.

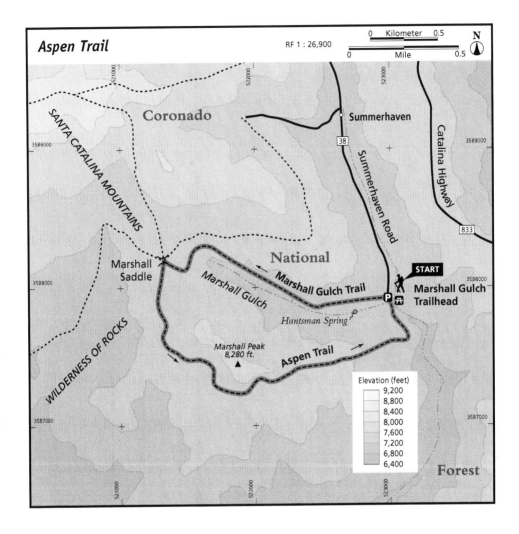

DIFFICULTY: Moderate.

PERMITTED USES: Hiking, horseback riding.

MAPS: Pusch Ridge Wilderness USFS.

SPECIAL CONSIDERATIONS: None.

PARKING AND FACILITIES: The trailhead is located at the Marshall Gulch Picnic Area, which has restrooms and parking.

FINDING THE TRAILHEAD: From the Sabino Canyon Visitor Center, turn left on Sabino Canyon Road, drive south 4.4 miles, and then turn left on Tanque Verde Road. Drive east 2.6 miles and then turn left on Catalina Highway. Stay on the Catalina Highway (a fee is required, payable at the entrance station a few miles into the mountains) 37.9

Wilderness of Rocks from the Aspen Trail, Santa Catalina Mountains

miles and then turn left on Summerhaven Road. Drive 1.7 miles south through Summerhaven to the end of the road at the Marshall Gulch Trailhead.

From the trailhead, start the hike on the Marshall Gulch Trail, which ascends Marshall Gulch west past Huntsman Spring to Marshall Saddle and a multiple-trail junction. Take the leftmost trail, the Aspen Trail, which heads south around Marshall Peak. There is an exceptionally good viewpoint on the small hill just southwest of the trail at 1.6 miles. From this vantage you can see much of the well-named Wilderness of Rocks to the southwest. Continue the hike on the Aspen Trail, which heads east as it continues around Marshall Peak, then descends a ridge to return to the Marshall Gulch Trailhead.

MILES AND DIRECTIONS

0.0 Start at the Marshall Gulch Trailhead.

1.2 At Marshall Saddle, turn left on the Aspen Trail.

1.6 Arrive at an exceptionally good viewpoint.

3.0 Return to the Marshall Gulch Trailhead.

Wilderness of Rocks Loop

HIGHLIGHTS: A long day hike or overnight backpack trip from Mount Lemmon through the scenic Wilderness of Rocks.

TYPE OF TRIP: Loop.

DISTANCE: 7.4 miles.

DIFFICULTY: Difficult.

PERMITTED USES: Hiking, horseback riding.

MAPS: Pusch Ridge Wilderness USFS.

SPECIAL CONSIDERATIONS: This trail starts at the top of Mount Lemmon and loses 2,800 feet of elevation, all of which you will have to climb at the end of the hike.

PARKING AND FACILITIES: The trailhead is a dirt parking area without facilities.

FINDING THE TRAILHEAD: From the Sabino Canyon Visitor Center, turn left on Sabino Canyon Road, drive south 4.4 miles, and then turn left on Tanque Verde Road. Drive east 2.6 miles and then turn left on Catalina Highway. Stay on the Catalina Highway (a fee is required,

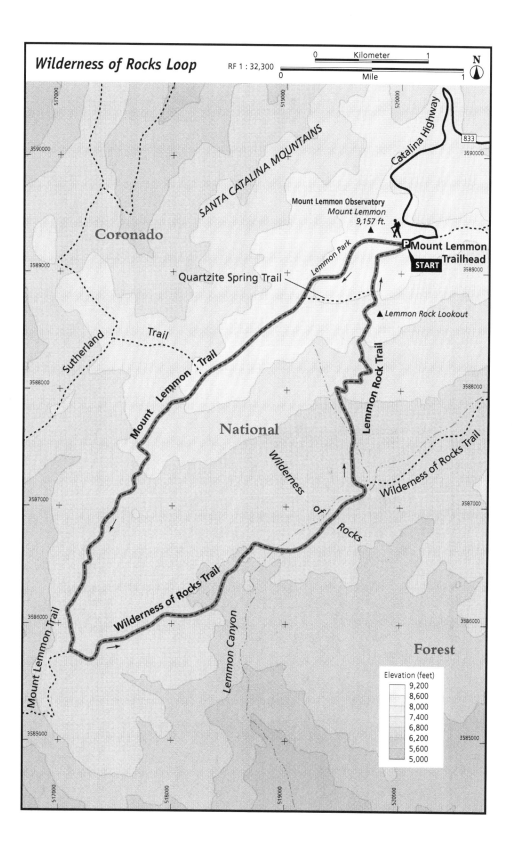

Wilderness of Rocks Loop

RF 1 : 32,300

Kilometer 0 — 1
Mile 0 — 1

N

SANTA CATALINA MOUNTAINS

Catalina Highway

833

Coronado

Mount Lemmon Observatory
Mount Lemmon
9,157 ft.
▲

Lemmon Park

P **Mount Lemmon Trailhead**
START

Quartzite Spring Trail

▲ *Lemmon Rock Lookout*

Sutherland

Trail

Mount Lemmon Trail

Lemmon Rock Trail

National

Wilderness

of

Rocks

Wilderness of Rocks Trail

Wilderness of Rocks Trail

Lemmon Canyon

Mount Lemmon Trail

Forest

Elevation (feet)
9,200
8,600
8,000
7,400
6,800
6,200
5,600
5,000

payable at the entrance station a few miles into the mountains) 40.4 miles to the end of the road at Mount Lemmon.

From the parking area, head west on the Mount Lemmon Trail, which skirts around the south side of the fenced Mount Lemmon Observatory, then heads southwest, descending on a broad ridge crest. You'll pass through Lemmon Park, which is a small meadow set in stands of ponderosa pine, Douglas fir, limber pine, and white fir, and then pass the junction with the Quartzite Spring Trail, where a powerline also meets the trail.

Those hikers wanting an easy hike can turn left here and hike 0.3 mile to the Lemmon Rock Trail. From this junction you could turn right and walk 0.2 mile to Lemmon Rock Lookout for the view, then backtrack to the junction and walk 0.3 mile to the Mount Lemmon Trailhead. The total distance of this loop is 1.7 miles.

To stay on the main loop, stay right on the Mount Lemmon Trail and follow it southwest down the ridge and along the powerline. Both the Sutherland Trail and the powerline leave the ridge to the west; stay left on the Mount Lemmon Trail. For about half a mile, the descent becomes steeper as the Mount Lemmon Trail drops down in a series of swtichbacks, then levels out and works its way around several hills along the ridge. A final descent leads to a saddle and the Wilderness of Rocks Trail.

Turn left on the Wilderness of Rocks Trail and follow it east and northeast into the headwaters of Lemmon Canyon. This area is known as the Wilderness of Rocks because of the large number of granite outcrops in the area. Mixed in with the ponderosa-pine–Gambel-oak forest, the rocks provide a delightful setting. Just east of the saddle, the trail descends to cross an unnamed tributary of Lemmon Canyon and climbs gradually over a broad ridge. A steeper, longer descent leads across another tributary. After this crossing, the Wilderness of Rocks Trail works its way across another broad ridge before dropping into upper Lemmon Canyon, which it follows to the junction with the Lemmon Rock Trail.

Turn left here and follow the Lemmon Rock Trail north. At first the trail climbs gradually, but soon the steep slopes of Mount Lemmon force the trail into a series of switchbacks. A huge rock outcrop to the west of the trail is called Rappel Rock because of the 200-foot overhang that allows climbers to do a long, free rappel. More switchbacks through the pine-and-oak forest lead to Lemmon Rock Lookout and one of the best views found anywhere in the Catalinas. A fire lookout building is staffed during high fire dangers and commands a view of much of the Pusch Ridge Wilderness, including the Wilderness of Rocks that you've just traversed, as well as the Santa Catalina Front Range. In the distance you can see the Rincon, Santa Rita, Baboquivari, and Tucson Mountains, among many others.

Continue north on the Lemmon Rock Trail, passing the Quartzite Spring Trail that comes in from the left. Follow the Lemmon Rock Trail up the final slopes to the Mount Lemmon Trailhead.

MILES AND DIRECTIONS

0.0 Start at the Mount Lemmon Trailhead.

0.7 Stay right at the Quartzite Spring Trail.

1.4 Stay left at the Sutherland Trail.

3.2 Turn left on Wilderness of Rocks Trail.

5.4 Turn left on Lemmon Rock Trail.

6.9 Arrive at Lemmon Rock Lookout.

7.1 Pass the Quartzite Spring Trail junction.

7.4 Arrive back at the Mount Lemmon Trailhead.

Tucson

aguaro National Park is unique in that it straddles a major city, one whose founding dates back to the early days of the settlement of North America. As you would expect, there are quite a few cultural attractions in and around Tucson. In this chapter I describe selected attractions you might want to visit in between your explorations of the park.

Arizona–Sonora Desert Museum

The Arizona–Sonora Desert Museum is a world-renowned natural history museum and botanical garden. Mountain lions, prairie dogs, Gila monsters, coyotes, black bears, javelina, and other animals are displayed in enclosures that re-create their beautiful Sonoran Desert habitat. Two miles of paths, much of which is wheelchair accessible, traverse twenty-one acres of museum grounds. On display are more than 300 animal species and 1,200 kinds of plants. If you plan to visit the museum before visiting the national park, you'll feel like you're hiking among old friends as you recognize plants from the museum.

A private, nonprofit organization dedicated to the conservation of the Sonoran Desert, the mission of the Arizona–Sonora Desert Museum is to inspire people to live in harmony with the natural world by fostering love, appreciation, and understanding of the Sonoran Desert. The museum not only

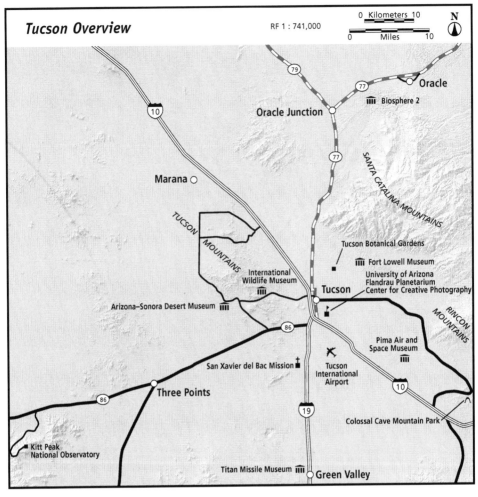

displays animals and plants of the desert, it also has educational, research, and conservation programs.

To reach the museum from Interstate 10, exit at Speedway and turn west. Speedway Boulevard becomes Gates Pass Road and enters Tucson Mountain Park. Turn right on Kinney Road and drive 2.5 miles north to the museum entrance, on the left. Gates Pass Road is not suitable for RVs or trailers.

From Interstate 19, exit at Ajo Way (Arizona Highway 86) and drive west to Kinney Road. Turn right and drive 7.5 miles north to the museum entrance.

Arizona–Sonora Desert Museum
2021 North Kinney Road
Tucson, AZ 85743
(520) 883–2702
www.desertmuseum.org

The Mexican gray wolf once ranged over southern Arizona and has recently been reintroduced in eastern Arizona. This wolf is at the Arizona–Sonora Desert Museum.

Biosphere 2

Founded in 1991 by John Allen, Biosphere 2 was originally intended to be a closed environment where human crews would live sealed inside for up to two years. Everything inside, including water, food, and air, would be recycled, modeling as closely as possible the kind of habitat humans might have to build to live in space or on other planets. The researchers regarded the Earth's biosphere as the first one, hence the name Biosphere 2 for the research facility. Unfortunately the crew of eight had to spend most of their time solving problems with the habitat and weren't able to do much scientific research. Unexplained low oxygen levels required extra air to be pumped in from outside, and numerous other violations of the experiment's supposedly sealed environment took place. Administrative wrangling added to Biosphere 2's problems. In 1996 Columbia University, which had been consulted on the oxygen problem, was brought in to manage the facility, seeing research potential that could help in studying the Earth's ecosystems, global warming, and other environmental issues. Although human crews have not been sealed inside since the original missions ended in 1994, future sealed missions are possible.

Biosphere 2 has a new visitor center and gift shop and offers guided tours through the three-acre glass-enclosed facility.

From Tucson, drive north on Arizona Highway 77, the Oracle Highway, to Biosphere 2.

Biosphere 2
32540 South Biosphere Road
Oracle, AZ 85623
(520) 838–6200
www.bio2.com

Center for Creative Photography

The Center for Creative Photography is an archive, museum, and research center dedicated to photography as an art form and cultural record. The center's collection is the nation's largest collection of works by twentieth-century North American photographers, including Ansel Adams, Lola Alvarez Bravo, Richard Avedon, Louise Dahl-Wolfe, W. Eugene Smith, and Edward Weston. The collection includes photographs, negatives, albums, work prints, manuscripts, audiovisual material, contact sheets, correspondence, and memorabilia totaling more than 60,000 works by 2,000 photographers.

Exhibits change every few months, and in addition, individuals can use the center's extensive library and make appointments to view prints from specific collections. The center also has a store with one of the largest collections of photography books in the country—more than 800 titles—in addition to posters, postcards, and the like.

The Center for Creative Photography is located in the Fine Arts complex in the northwest corner of the University of Arizona campus, between the Architecture and Harvill buildings. Pay parking is available at the Park Avenue Garage on the northeast corner of Park and Speedway.

To reach the center from I–10, exit at Speedway Boulevard and turn east. Drive 1.5 miles to Park Avenue, then turn left and then immediately right into the Park Avenue Garage. Walk to the pedestrian underpass at the southeast corner of the garage, which will take you under Speedway Boulevard. The center is the second building on your left, between Architecture and Harvill.

Center for Creative Photography
The University of Arizona
1030 North Olive Road
PO Box 210103
Tucson, AZ 85721
(520) 621–7968
http://dizzy.library.arizona.edu/branches/ccp/home/home.html

Colossal Cave Mountain Park

Colossal Cave is the primary attraction at privately owned Colossal Cave Mountain Park. Available daily all year, the guided tour is about 0.5-mile long and takes about forty-five minutes to complete. Because the temperature inside the cave stays at seventy degrees F year-round, a cave tour is a great thing to do on a hot summer day. Cave formations include stalagmites, stalactites, box work, flowstone, and helictites. The guide explains these features as well as the history and geology of the cave and park.

From Tucson, take Broadway Road east to Old Spanish Trail, turn right, and then drive about 17 miles to Colossal Cave.

Wild turkey on exhibit at the Arizona–Sonora Desert Museum

From I–10 east of Tucson, exit onto Vail Road, turn north, and follow signs for about 56 miles.

Colossal Cave Mountain Park
16721 East Old Spanish Trail
PO Box 70
Vail, AZ 85641
(520) 647–7275
www.colossalcave.com

Flandrau Science Center and Planetarium

The centerpiece of the Flandrau Center is, of course, the planetarium. A thirty-projector system displays 8,600 objects, including stars, galaxies, planets, the sun and moon, and meteors on the 50-foot dome. Planetarium shows change regularly. For information, call the number below or visit the center's Web site.

Using a 16-inch cassegrain telescope, the center's observatory offers free viewing to the public Wednesday through Saturday evenings about an hour after sunset.

The center also operates a mineral museum with one of the largest university-owned mineral collections in the country. Of special interest is the meteorite collection, including pieces of the Diablo Canyon Meteorite that formed Arizona's Meteor Crater.

There's also a science store, with related gifts and other items.

Flandrau Center is located on the campus of the University of Arizona, at the corner of Cherry and University Boulevard.

Flandrau Science Center
1601 East University Boulevard
Tucson, AZ 85719
(520) 621–7827
www.flandrau.org

Fort Lowell Museum

The museum is located in the reconstructed commanding officer's quarters of Fort Lowell, which was established in 1873. The museum, operated by the Arizona Historical Society, focuses on military life on the Arizona frontier. Special events include walking tours, lectures, and living-history events.

Camp Lowell was established in 1866 by the U.S. Army on the outskirts of Tucson, but in 1873 the post was moved 7 miles northeast. Fort Lowell had several missions, including guarding wagon trains and supplies, protecting settlers, patrolling the Mexican border, and conducting offensive operations against the Apache Indians. An average of 130 officers and 239 enlisted men served at the fort.

Constructed in the classic Sonoran style, the buildings at Fort Lowell reflected the hot, arid climate. Thick adobe walls and wide hallways were roofed with pine logs and saguaro cactus ribs and a thick layer of dirt. Such construction keeps the interior relatively cool in summer and warm in winter. Nearby Tucson provided the troops with diversions such as dances, saloons, gambling halls, dinners, and baseball games. After the Apache wars ended with the capture of Geronimo and his band, the army saw no further need for Fort Lowell and abandoned the post in 1891.

From I–10, exit at Grant Road and turn east. Drive 7 miles, turn left on Craycroft Road, and continue 0.6 mile north to Old Fort Lowell Park.

Fort Lowell Museum
2900 North Craycroft Road
Tucson, AZ 85712
(520) 885–3832

International Wildlife Museum

Founded in 1988, the International Wildlife Museum has collections that are more than one hundred years old, including more than 400 kinds of birds, insects, and mammals from around the world. The collection is exhibited in realistic, natural settings in a building modeled after an old adobe French Foreign Legion fort in Chad, Africa. Interactive computers and hands-on exhibits help make the museum fun and educational for visitors of all ages. Wildlife films are shown on the hour in the state-of-the-art theater.

From I–10 in Tucson, take the Speedway exit west. Speedway Boulevard becomes Gates Pass Road, and the museum is 5 miles west of I–10.

International Wildlife Museum
4800 Gates Pass Road
Tucson, AZ 85745
(520) 629–0100
www.thewildlifemuseum.org

Kitt Peak National Observatory

Kitt Peak, on the Tohono O'odham Reservation southwest of Tucson, is home to the world's largest collection of optical telescopes, as well as two radio telescopes. Dozens of astronomical research institutions are active on this observing site, which is operated by the National Optical Astronomy Observatory. The observatory has a visitor center and gift shop, as well as guided and self-guided tours. You can also observe the night sky yourself using the visitor center's 16-inch telescope. Nightly stargazing groups are limited and reservations are required well in advance.

To reach Kitt Peak from Tucson, take the AZ 86 exit (Ajo Way) from I–10 or I–19 44 miles to Arizona Highway 386. Turn left and drive 12 miles to the Kitt Peak Visitor Center.

Kitt Peak National Observatory
State Route 86 (Ajo Way)
Sells, AZ 85634
(520) 318–8726
www.noao.edu/kpno

Pima Air and Space Museum

The largest privately owned air and space museum in the world, the Pima Air and Space Museum now has more than 250 aircraft displayed on eighty acres of land and in several large buildings. Although the museum emphasizes military aircraft due to its location next to the Aerospace Maintenance and Regeneration Center at Davis Monthan Air Force Base, it also houses civilian aircraft, including a full-size replica of the first Wright Flyer and an Air Force One used by Presidents Eisenhower and Kennedy. Other aircraft include one of the B-52 bombers modified to carry the X-15 rocket plane and the fastest manned aircraft ever built, the SR-71 Blackbird spy plane.

From I-10 in Tucson, exit at Valencia Road and turn east. Drive 2 miles to the museum entrance.

Pima Air and Space Museum
6000 East Valencia Road
Tucson, AZ 85706
(520) 574–0462
www.pimaair.org

San Xavier del Bac Mission

San Xavier del Bac Mission is located in the Santa Cruz Valley 9 miles south of Tucson. Often called the "white dove of the desert," the brilliant white dome, towers, and spires stand out against the mesquite-covered desert floor, brown hills, and bright blue sky.

Since before the arrival of the Spanish, the Tohono O'odham settlement here was called "Bac," meaning "place where the water appears." The Santa Cruz River, which flows intermittently, reappears on the surface nearby. Father Eusebio Francisco Kino, the famous Spanish missionary and explorer, first vis-

Rincon Peak from Reef Rock, Rincon Mountains

ited Bac in 1692. In 1700 Father Kino laid the foundations of the first church, about 2 miles north of the present mission. He named it San Xavier in honor of his chosen patron, St. Francis Xavier, the Jesuit "Apostle of the Indies." In 1768 Fray Francisco Hermengildo Garces, a Franciscan friar of many accomplishments in Arizona, established his headquarters at San Xavier and used it as a base for his many missionary explorations.

Built from 1783 to 1797 by Franciscan Fathers Juan Bautista Velderrain and Juan Bautista Llorenz, the present church is a graceful blend of Moorish, Byzantine, and late Mexican Renaissance architecture. San Xavier Mission is widely regarded as the finest example of mission architecture in the United States. No one knows who the architect was or how the church was built, and the fact that one tower was never completed remains a mystery to this day. Clearly the local Tohono O'odham people played a major role in the construction.

A series of domes and arches creates enclaves for paintings on the various walls, domes, and rooms. The paintings are original, but the harsh desert climate has taken its toll and restoration work is an ongoing process. The outside of the church requires even more maintenance, and a fund has been set up for that purpose.

San Xavier del Bac Mission is a fully functioning parish church within the Diocese of Tucson, still run by the Franciscan friars after more than 200 years. The church primarily serves the Tohono O'odham but is open to all.

From I–10 in Tucson, drive south on I–19 6.1 miles, exit on San Xavier Road, turn right, and drive 1.2 miles to the mission.

San Xavier del Bac Mission
1950 West San Xavier Road
Tucson, AZ 85746
(520) 294–2624
www.sanxaviermission.org

Titan Missile Museum

A chilling reminder of the tensions of the cold war, the Titan Missile Museum is the only remaining underground missile silo left from the original eighteen sites located around Tucson. A total of fifty-four Titan missile sites were operational from 1964 to 1984.

The Titan is a liquid-fueled intercontinental ballistic missile capable of delivering a nuclear warhead 8,000 miles. Manned by highly trained and dedicated air force crews, the complex consisted of the missile in its underground silo, an underground control center, and an access portal. Designed to withstand anything but a direct hit with a nuclear weapon, each missile site could fire its weapon in one minute after receipt of the launch order. When the United States and the Soviet Union agreed on the elimination of the Titan missiles as part of a treaty to reduce nuclear arms on both sides, the missiles were removed and modified to launch weather and communication satellites, a mission they are still performing. Equipment was salvaged from the other fifty-three Titan sites before the silos were destroyed. The air force turned over the site now containing the Titan Missile Museum to the Pima Air and Space Museum.

Although the missile in the museum's silo was a training missile that was never fueled, you can see the steps that were required so the Soviet government could verify that the missile complied with the terms of the treaty. One of the two massive concrete blast doors that used to cover the silo was fixed in the closed position, and the other, open half of the silo is covered with a glass skylight. Holes were cut in the warhead nose cone so that satellites could verify that it was empty.

The museum has exhibits, archives and research materials, and a gift shop. An underground guided tour takes you to the missile silo and the control center, where a tape is played of a simulated launch.

From I–10 in Tucson, drive south on I–19 to Duval Mine Road and exit. Turn right and go 0.1 mile west to the museum entrance.

Titan Missile Museum
1580 West Duval Mine Road
Sahuarita, AZ 85629
(520) 625–7736
www.pimaair.org/TitanMM/titanhome.shtml

Tucson Botanical Gardens

Located in central Tucson, Tucson Botanical Gardens is a five-acre collection of sixteen specialty gardens including the Backyard Bird Garden, Butterfly Garden, Cactus and Succulent Garden, Children's Discovery Garden, Herb Garden, Historical Gardens, Iris Garden, Native American Crops Garden, Jardín (Our Garden), Plants of the Tohono O'odham Path, Sensory Garden, Kay's Shade Garden, Tropical Exhibit, Wildflower Garden, and the Xeriscape Demonstration Garden. Consisting of more than 4,200 individual plants, the gardens offer many design ideas for residential gardens using the wide variety of plants that thrive in southern Arizona.

The Tucson Botanical Gardens offers tours and classes and puts on special events.

From I–10 in Tucson, exit at Grant Road and drive 4.8 miles east. Turn right on Alvernon Way and go 0.1 mile to the gardens, on the left.

Tucson Botanical Gardens
2150 North Alvernon Way
Tucson, AZ 85712
(520) 326–9686
www.tucsonbotanical.org

Appendix A
For More Information

Coronado National Forest
Supervisors Office
300 West Congress Street
Tucson, AZ 85701
(520) 670–4552
www.fs.fed.us/r3/coronado/

Coronado National Forest
Santa Catalina Ranger District
5700 North Sabino Canyon Road
Tucson, AZ 85750
(520) 749–8700
www.fs.fed.us/r3/coronado/

Ironwood Forest National
  Monument
Bureau of Land Management
Tucson Field Office
12661 East Broadway Road
Tucson, AZ 85748
(520) 258–7200
www.az.blm.gov/ironwood/
  ironwood.htm

Saguaro National Park
Headquarters and Rincon Mountain
  District
3693 South Old Spanish Trail
Tucson, AZ 85730
(520) 733–5153
www.nps.gov/sagu

Saguaro National Park
Tucson Mountain District
2700 North Kinney Road
Tucson, AZ 85743
(520) 733–5158

Tucson Mountain Park
3500 West River Road
Tucson, AZ 85741
(520) 877–6000
www.co.pima.az.us/pksrec/natres/
  tucmts/tumtpk.html

Appendix B
Resources

Arnberger, Leslie Preston. *Flowers of the Southwest Mountains.* Tucson, Ariz.: Southwest Parks and Monuments Association, 1982.

Bailey, John, and Laura Walters. *Tucson Dayhikers Guide.* Tucson, Ariz.: Muddy Creek Crafts, 2002.

Bowers, Janice Emily. *Shrubs and Trees of the Southwest Deserts.* Tucson, Ariz.: Western National Parks Association, 1993.

Cowgill, Pete, and Eber Glendenning. *Santa Catalina Mountains: A Guide to the Trails and Routes.* Tucson, Ariz.: Rainbow Expeditions, 1997.

Dodge, Natt Noyes. *Flowers of the Southwest Deserts.* Tucson, Ariz.: Western National Parks Assocation, 1985.

Elmore, Francis H. *Shrubs and Trees of the Southwest Uplands.* Tucson, Ariz.: Western National Parks Association, 1976.

Green, Stewart M. *Rock Climbing Arizona.* Guilford, Conn.: Globe Pequot Press, 1999.

Grubbs, Bruce. *Camping Arizona.* Guilford, Conn.: Globe Pequot Press, 1999.

Grubbs, Bruce. *Desert Hiking Tips.* Guilford, Conn.: Globe Pequot Press, 1998.

Grubbs, Bruce. *Using GPS: GPS Simplified for Outdoor Adventures.* Guilford, Conn.: Globe Pequot Press, 1999.

Grubbs, Bruce, and Stewart Aitchison. *Hiking Arizona.* Guilford, Conn.: Globe Pequot Press, 2002.

Hare, Trevor. *Poisonous Dwellers of the Desert.* Tucson, Ariz.: Western National Parks Association, 1995.

Harmon, Will. *Leave No Trace.* Guilford, Conn.: Globe Pequot Press, 1997.

Houk, Rose. *Sonoran Desert.* Tucson, Ariz.: Western National Parks Association, 2000.

Leavengood, Betty. *Tucson Hiking Guide.* Boulder, Colo.: Pruett Publishing, 1997.

Lucchitta, Ivo. *Hiking Arizona's Geology.* Seattle: The Mountaineers Books, 2001.

McGiveney, Annette. *Leave No Trace: A Guide to the New Wilderness Etiquette.* Seattle: The Mountaineers Books, 2003.

Molvar, Eric. *Hiking Arizona's Cactus Country.* Guilford, Conn.: Globe Pequot Press, 2000.

Mullally, Linda. *Hiking with Dogs.* Guilford, Conn.: Globe Pequot Press, 1999.

Olin, George. *House in the Sun: A Natural History of the Sonoran Desert.* Tucson, Ariz.: Western National Parks Association, 1994.

Pusch Ridge Wilderness. U.S. Forest Service, 1997.

Saguaro National Park. Washington, DC: National Geographic Maps, 2000.

Spellenberg, Richard. *Sonoran Desert Wildflowers.* Guilford, Conn.: Globe Pequot Press, 2002.

Tawney, Robin. *Hiking with Kids.* Guilford, Conn.: Globe Pequot Press, 2000.

Warren, Scott S. *100 Classic Hikes in Arizona.* Seattle: The Mountaineers Books, 2000.

Weir, Bill. *Moon Handbooks: Arizona.* Emeryville, Calif.: Avalon Travel Publishing, 2002.

Weiss, Eric. *Wilderness 911: A Step-by-Step Guide for Medical Emergencies and Improvised Care in the Backcountry.* Seattle: The Mountaineers Books, 1998.

Wilkerson, James A. *Medicine for Mountaineering and Other Wilderness Activities.* Seattle: The Mountaineers Books, 2001.

Index

About the Author

Bruce Grubbs is an avid camper, backpacker, hiker, mountain biker, paddler, and cross-country skier who has been exploring the American desert for more than thirty-five years. He lives in Flagstaff, Arizona, where he flies charters and fixes computers in addition to writing and photographing the outdoors. His other Falcon books include:

Hiking Arizona (with Stewart Aitchison)

Hiking Northern Arizona

Best Easy Day Hikes Flagstaff

Best Easy Day Hikes Sedona

Camping Arizona

Hiking Arizona's Superstition and Mazatal County

Mountain Biking Phoenix

Mountain Biking Flagstaff and Sedona

Using GPS: GPS Simplified for Outdoor Adventures

Desert Hiking Tips

Hiking Nevada

Hiking Great Basin National Park

Hiking Oregon's Central Cascades

Mountain Biking St. George and Cedar City

For more information, check the author's Web site at www.brucegrubbs.com.